COMPLETE BOOK

OF

MODEL BUSINESS LETTERS

COMPLETE BOOK
OF
MODEL BUSINESS LETTERS

Martha W. Cresci

PARKER PUBLISHING COMPANY, Inc.
WEST NYACK, NEW YORK

To Mabel George, who set my feet
on the writer's path so long ago.

© 1976 *by*

Parker Publishing Company, Inc.
West Nyack, New York

Library of Congress Cataloging in Publication Data

Cresci, Martha W
   Complete book of model business letters.

   Includes index.
   1. Commercial correspondence. 2. Form letters.
I. Title.
HF5726.C85   651.7'5   75-43646
ISBN 0-13-157438-8

Printed in the United States of America

How You Can Use This Book Daily to Solve Letter-Writing Problems

We have only to think of the enormous increase in postal volume each year to realize how vital letters are to modern business. They are the crux of communication, verification and permanent records. They represent billions of dollars spent in commerce and industry, and all of us are aware that a letter can make or break an effective relationship with a customer or other important contact. Yet many letters must be rushed out. Very often there is simply not enough time to think out the perfect solution to a letter problem, and the writer ends up having to exchange three or four letters, rather than having one letter do the job.

Precious time and money, big money, are involved. Stop and estimate now just how many letters there are in your company's files. Official studies show that the average cost of each business letter is over $3, with the figure climbing year by year. Represented are the hourly cost of your time, the secretary's time, clerical time, plus cost of equipment, stationery and postage. Rather staggering, when you compute it.

It was with these thoughts in mind that this book was researched and written. Time, the biggest item in letter cost, can be cut 'way down with the use of this book.

A study of thousands of business letters revealed there *are* special techniques that can be applied for success in letter-writing. Moreover, it became apparent that business letters fall into categories, so they can be classified, and the good ones used as models.

5

No longer will you have to wrack your brain for a good beginning, or search desperately for a graceful way to express an awkward thought. Your letter-writing time, the major cost factor, will be cut to a minimum. Moreover, you will be happier with the finished product . . . and much happier with the *results* of your well-written letters.

How to Reap These Benefits

With over 275 actual letters included in this book, covering scores of categories, you are practically certain to find an expertly written letter for the situation that confronts you. You have only to change a word or so here and there to personalize that letter and make it fit your purpose exactly.

An Example of How to Do It

For example, take the following letter about a mixup in an order for ceramic bowls. You can make this fit a problem of your own, by simply changing details. Let us say you have ordered a total of 10 boxes of 1000 white wove envelopes: six boxes of size 4 1/8" x 9½" and four boxes of size 3 5/8" x 6½". When they arrive you find that the quantities have been reversed, with your receiving 4 boxes of the large size and 6 boxes of the small size. Here is model letter #1 revised to cover this situation:

      Your address
      Your city, state, and zip code
      Date

Mr. James Farber, Order Dept.
XYZ Envelope Co.
Street Address
City, State and Zip Code

    Our Order No.:3719115
    Your Invoice No.:WWE44223921

Dear Mr. Farber:

On June 15th we sent you an order for 10 boxes of White Wove Envelopes, 6 boxes to be #3219, size 4 1/8" x 9½"; and 4 boxes to be #2219, size 3 5/8" x 6½".

When we received the order we discovered that the quantities had been reversed on the two sizes, without explanation, and this is not satisfactory.

Please ship'us immediately 2 more boxes of the larger envelopes #3219 White Wove, @ $13.90. PLEASE RUSH.

We are returning for credit the extra two boxes of envelopes #2219, which we did not order. They are being sent to you via United Parcel, and were shipped today, June 26, marked for your attention.

We are in urgent need of the larger envelopes, as they are to be used for a special mailing piece that is to go out two weeks from now. Anything you can do to expedite correction of the error will be greatly appreciated. Our Order No. was 3719115. Your Invoice No. was WWE44223921.

Very truly yours,

If your error situation were simpler—if, for instance, you had ordered 10 boxes of envelopes in the larger size and been sent 10 boxes of the wrong size, you could adapt this same letter. You would merely omit the portions of the model letter that do not apply. For a less formal approach you might use letters #2 or #3 (Chapter 1) covering the same sort of situation.

Key Factors in a Good Business Letter

Ninety-nine per cent of the time a good letter should be short and to the point, yet courteous. No one should have to waste time digging out the message from a mass of verbiage. The letter's simple wording, its directness, and even its physical appearance should help the reader get the message immediately. In many cases the letter should point toward a required action, and speed the taking of this action. A good letter, at the same time, should create a feeling of cooperativeness and good will in the person it is addressed to. Acerbic letters may be fun to write occasionally, but all of them, in a business framework, should be consigned to the wastebasket.

Keep in mind when you read the letters in this book, and when you write your own, that the best modern letter-writing is conversational in tone. There is no place for stilted phrases or archaic forms. Write your message just as you would tell it, editing for brevity, and designing the physical appearance of the letter to help get your message across. (See page 274 in Chapter 15 for more about the physical arrangement of letters.)

True, some well-written letters are graceful, some may even have a touch of humor; but by and large good letters need not possess these characteristics. There is no point in having the reader exclaim over your literary skill, or stand in awe of your vocabulary, if he ends up wondering what on earth you are talking about—and then does the wrong thing in response! Insurance snafus, mistakes in orders, merchandise returns . . . the mere mention of these brings to almost anyone's mind some horrendous memories of what unskilled letter-writing can bring about in misunderstanding and time-wasting.

The Purpose of This Book Is to Be Immediately USEFUL

The world is replete with wordy books that purport to teach letterwriting—but give you few examples. *The Complete Book of Model Business Letters* is filled with actual LETTERS, letters you can seize upon and use. The teaching part is secondary—pithy, direct, and to the point. As you use these tested, successful letters, over the months and years, you are bound to become quite an expert yourself; but you do not have to be one. This book, right from the beginning, will help you write letters that *get results.*

Martha W. Cresci

ACKNOWLEDGMENTS

My thanks to the many persons who furnished some of the raw materials for this book. Special thanks to James Bie, Herbert Boynton, Charles Glenn, Alexandra Guffey, Jana Joseph, Roger Leonard, Jean McArthur, John Ona, Norman Pos, Walter Reynolds, Rae Weatherly, Barbara Whitney, Nathan R. Wilson and William Wilson.

M. W. C.

CONTENTS

Letters Asking for Information *(Continued)*

Models for Letters of Acceptance and Refusal *(Continued)*

Personal Letters in a Business Framework *(Continued)*

CHAPTER 1

How to Write Letters That

Straighten Out Errors and Mix-ups

Among the most difficult of letters to write are those that attempt to straighten out errors. Unless they are carefully and skillfully written, they sometimes compound the original error, or lead to new ones, and a monster snarl wastes time and frays the tempers of everyone concerned.

There are several rules to keep in mind if you hope to head off this sort of development.

1. Keep your temper. Nothing is gained by making the "opposition" angry.
2. Before you begin to write or dictate, be clear in your own mind as to the details of the situation and what you wish to say. Do not dwell too much on details of the error, but *emphasize the desired solution.*
3. Write to a *person,* not a box number or a department. This becomes increasingly important as computer use multiplies in business. If you know someone in the organization by name, no matter what his job, address your letter to him and ask him to forward it to the proper person. If you do not know anyone by name, at least address the letter to someone—the Chief Shipping Clerk; Manager, Complaint Dept.; or any title you think appropriate to the case.
4. Make the form of the letter assist in clarifying the problem. Consider using tabulation and underlining to make it easy for the recipient to get your point or points.

5. Highlight, underline and repeat identifying numbers—job numbers, invoice numbers, model numbers, etc. Make it impossible for the reader to miss what you are talking about. (Remember that your letter will often be passed on to a clerk or subordinate, with a vague order to "straighten this out." Proper emphasis makes it easy for him to do so.)
6. Keep your letter as simple as possible. Make it brief, but not so brief as to be curt or rude.
7. Enclose copies of any documents referred to, but keep the originals.
8. In returning merchandise send a letter to the person involved, and make sure to enclose a copy of your letter and copies of related documents with the merchandise itself. If originals must be sent, be sure to keep photocopies.

Choose one of the following letters that most nearly fits your situation and substitute your own facts. The model letters given proceed from fairly simple errors to complex snarls.

Asking Correction of Simple Error

Note how the arrangement of the letters and a careful use of underlining clarify the problem. Repetition is used deliberately in some cases to emphasize a point.

#1   (Letterhead)

October 22, 19___

Mr. Raymond Brown, Sales Dept.
Hardgoods Mfr.
749 Fairmount Ave.
Urbanville, Mass. 00000

Our Order No.: 105967
Your Invoice No.: 2037492

Dear Mr. Brown:

On October 8th we sent you an order for a number of assorted items for our Pre-Christmas Sale. Among them was listed 2 dozen Ceramic Bowls, #71 @ $60 per dozen, 6 blue, 6 red, and 12 yellow.

When we received the order we discovered that all two dozen bowls had been sent to us in yellow, without explanation, and this is not satisfactory.

Please ship us immediately the 6 blue bowls and 6 red bowls, #71, specified in our order No. 105967.

We are returning for credit the extra dozen yellow bowls #71 which we did not order. They are being sent to you via Translines, and were shipped today, October 22, marked for your attention.

As you may remember, our Pre-Christmas Sale begins November 20th, and we should like to have all merchandise for the sale on hand well before that date. Anything you can do to expedite correction of the error on the bowls will be greatly appreciated. Our Order No. was 105967. Your Invoice No. was 2037492.

Very truly yours,

Sam Jones, Housewares Buyer
Anystore, Inc.

Enc.

The above letter is the type you might send to someone you do not know personally or do not know very well. If you are friendly with Raymond Brown, your letter can be much less formal; but again, it should spotlight all the important numbers and facts. It is often a good idea to repeat something like the invoice number, as Sam Jones has done, to make doubly sure the correct document is referred to when the order is being corrected.

Here is an example of a similar problem being dealt with in much less formal letters:

#2   (Letterhead)

October 22, 19___

Mr. Raymond Brown, Sales Dept.
Hardgoods Mfr.
749 Fairmount Ave.
Urbanville, Mass. 00000

<u>Our Order No.</u>: 409764
<u>Your Invoice No.</u>: 3946423

Dear Brown:

You had better shake up that shipping department of yours. They have gotten me into a real mess on some of the Christmas merchandise. (I know it isn't your fault, because we discussed the order at length, and I saw you write it out.)

As you may remember, I was particularly anxious to have those Taiwan Ceramic Bowls in red and blue, as well as yellow, as those colors seem to be picking up in our area. So what do I get? All yellow! Please see what you can do to straighten this out in a hurry.

> <u>Please ship us immediately</u> the <u>6 blue</u> bowls and the <u>6 red</u>
> bowls, #71, which were specified in our order No. 409764.

We are returning for credit the extra dozen yellow bowls #71 which were not ordered. I can't use this many in yellow. They are being sent to you via Translines, and went out today, October 22, marked for your attention.

Please get the correct bowls off to us as soon as you can, Ray, as the red and blue were mentioned in the Christmas circular, which goes out November 18th. An idea— If you are going to be in this area again before that date, how about bringing them with you? It would save me some embarrassment. I am enclosing a photocopy of your invoice, and of our order. Hope to see you soon. Let me know what is being done.

With best personal regards,

Sam Jones, Housewares Buyer
Anystore, Inc.

Enc.

Another Informal Version

#3   (Letterhead)

October 22, 19___

Mr. Raymond Brown, Sales Dept.
Hardgoods Mfr.
749 Fairmount Ave.
Urbanville, Mass. 00000

Our Order No.: 409764
Your Invoice No.: 3946423

Dear Mr. Brown:

There has been a mix-up in my recent order for Christmas merchandise, and it is causing me difficulty and embarrassment. Some of the items are mentioned in our sale circular which goes out November 18th, and we do not have all the colors listed. I relied on your promise that all merchandise would be here in time, and I am catching hell for it. Will you please check into this matter yourself and rush the needed items to me?

I am referring to our order of October 8. Among the items ordered were 2 dozen Ceramic Bowls, #71 @ $60 per dozen, 6 blue, 6 red, and 12 yellow. When we received the order we discovered that all two dozen #71 bowls had been sent to us in yellow, without explanation. The extra dozen yellow bowls which we did not order will be returned to you for credit within a few days.

> Please ship us immediately the 6 blue bowls and the 6 red bowls, #71, specified in our order No. 409764.

I know you realize how important it is for us to have on hand all merchandise which we advertise. Anything you can do to speed these items to us will be greatly appreciated.

Yours truly,

Sam Jones, Housewares Buyer
Anystore, Inc.

A More Complex Situation Dealt With

#4

4721 Broadway
Urbanville, Ohio 00000
Sept. 21, 19___

Personnel Dept.
Nemo Corporation
900 Blank St.
St. Louis, Mo. 00000

Attention: Miss Joan Reynolds

Dear Sirs:

In our letter of September 15th we requested the work and health records of John R. Smith of Dept. 147, Kansas City. You sent us instead the work record of John R.V. Smith of Dept. 147—a different person. The health records sent were correct, but were incomplete, with the last 6 months missing.

The Material We Now Need Is:

1. Health Record of November through April of this year for John R. Smith of Dept. 147, Kansas City; Social Security No. 000-00-0000.
2. Complete Work Record of John R. Smith of Dept. 147, Kansas City; Social Security No. 000-00-0000.

Please rush the correct records to us by air mail, as we are urgently in need of them. Please double-check name and Social Security number. Upon receipt of the correct material, the records sent us by mistake will be returned to you.

Yours very truly,

John Doe, Supervisor
Dept. 992

In such a situation it is wise to state the mistake as briefly as possible, consistent with clarity, and get on to the correction of the error. With tabulation and a discreet use of underlining, try to make it impossible to miss the salient points. Try to picture how the person receiving the letter will use it. In this case the girl will probably take the letter to the files with her. By underlining the correct name only and the Social Security number, you make it easy for her to refer to them. By numbering your requests you remind her that there are two items needed.

If you have had trouble of this sort before, with this same clerk, you might even take a pen and bracket the section headed, "The Material We Now Need Is:".

Unless company rules force you to do so, it is wise not to return the incorrect material until you receive the proper records. It would just add to the things that the clerk would have to read and consider. And who knows, the same error might be committed again!

Proceed with caution where the use of underlining is concerned. Use it sparingly. Remember, if you underline everything, or almost everything, then nothing stands out.

Straightening Out a Really Bad Snarl

Some foul-ups can become unbelievably complicated, as everyone knows. The important thing in avoiding such situations is to make your original letter of complaint, or your request for change, as clear as you possibly can. In any complex situation, when errors do develop, realize that there is a potential of further errors adding to the snarl. Use classification, grouping, tabulation and occasional underlining to assist the reader in sorting out the facets of the problem. Test out the clarity of your letter by letting one or two other persons read it, and see if they can explain to you what it is that the recipient is to do.

Here is a letter that I wrote for a cosmetics saleswoman to help her straighten out a mess she had gotten into concerning returned merchandise. I did not see her original letter, but I imagine that she had not given it sufficient thought. It was also a mistake for her to have placed all these items in one package, without identifying the groups they belonged to. Be that as it may, the snarl was there when she came to me for help. The following letter we got together may help you to straighten out a similar situation. The quantities involved here are small, but the same treatment would apply to much larger shipments.

#5

3042 Near St.
Ourtown, Calif. 00000
July 14, 19___

Inhome Beauty Co.
1697 Far St.
Bigtown, N.J. 00000

Dear Sirs:

On May 4th I returned to you a collection of merchandise which consisted of four different groups. I realize that the situation was confusing and it was easy to make an error, but errors were made in the refunds, and I hope that you can straighten them out promptly. The four groups included in my returned goods shipment were as follows:

Group 1: Some merchandise turned over to me by Gretchen Brown, who formerly had this territory. Since she was leaving the city, she asked me to return this merchandise and to forward the refund to her when she sends me her address. The following items, returned for full credit at the regular price, were in Group 1:

		Amount Still Owed to Me:
3 4-ounce bottles of XYZ Spray Cologne @ $4.50	$13.50	
6 Asst. Soothie Lipsticks @ 80¢	4.80	
2 Bath Powder, Azalea and Spring Flowers, @ $3.00	6.00	
Total Due Me	$24.30	
Amount Refunded	$18.00	$6.30

Group 2: Two items at sale prices returned to me by customers.

1 bottle of Balm Lotion @ $4.50 less 40%	$ 2.70	
1 Zippy After Shave, flag bottle, @ $6.00 less 40%	3.60	
Amount due me	$ 6.30	
Amount refunded	$ 6.30	$0.00

Group 3: Damaged Sample Kit @ $10.00

Amount Refunded	$ 6.00	$4.00

Group 4: A good customer's DeLuxe Holiday Gift Kit returned to me because of allergy. (This was purchased at regular price and a Xerox of the sales slip is enclosed.) @ $29.50 less 40% 17.70

Amount due me $17.70
Amount refunded $15.00 $2.70

As you can see, I was shorted on the refund through some miscalculation, and it is causing me great inconvenience. I will certainly appreciate it if you will go over this transaction again and send me a check promptly.

TOTAL AMOUNT STILL OWED TO ME . . . $13.00

Yours very truly,

JANE DOE

Enc.

Dealing with Computer Errors

Human errors are bad enough to deal with, but as we all know, the computer age has ushered in an entirely new dimension to the state of utter confusion. Luckily, in the case of computer errors, you often get some kind of printout, so that you may be able to figure out where the error occurred. When you can do this you have won half the battle.

Following is an excellent letter written about a computer's mix-up of a mortgage payment record. Note that the letter is addressed to a person. This is vital. Never try to argue with a machine! If you do not have the name of a person in the company to write to, at least write to the director of some department. Make up a reasonable department name if you must; but never send the communication back in the return-envelope enclosed, or to the post office box from which it came. Send it to a street address.

Here is the letter, which is a useful model:

Locating the Error Yourself Helps Speed Correction

#6

3219 Nullo St.
Suburbia, Pa. 00000
July 10, 19___

Mr. John Willis
Mortgage Dept.
State National Bank
3012 North St.
New York, N.Y. 00000

Re: Mortgage on 3219 Nullo St., Suburbia, Pa.

Dear Mr. Willis:

On our latest mortgage statement I was startled to note that our payment had been greatly increased, which had to be an error, there being no reason for it. I knew, for one thing, that taxes in our area had been reduced, because of the great influx of businesses during the last year. A call to the County Tax Collector verified the fact that our taxes had indeed been reduced. Thus our payment should be lower rather than higher.

This being so, I decided to do a little detective work to see if I could find out the source of the error. A copy of the computer printout of the total charges and payments for the year had been sent us, so I went over this very carefully. I have enclosed copies of the papers mentioned so you can check my findings.

Going over the printout you will note that on Feb. 15 our taxes for 6 months were paid; then (five lines down) this same amount was again paid on March 10 (by mistake). Apparently the computer added these two payments together and took the total as our tax bill for six months. Thus a full year's taxes, $2,070.00, was added to our mortgage payment due for the next six months—when actually our full year's taxes have already been paid.

It appears that the amount we now owe is:

> $8070.00 minus $2070.00 in taxes already paid; or a net amount of $6000.00.

Please verify this and send me a corrected mortgage statement for the six months starting June 1, together with a corrected computer printout. I should like to send you a check and close our books for this month as soon as possible. Thank you for your assistance.

Yours very truly,

Sam E. Beaver
X-L Manufactures, Inc.

Enc.

Handling a Persistent Billing Error

This is another situation in which you must try to bypass the computer. Address your complaint to a person. If there is no name available, think up a title and a likely department, as: Manager, Customer Relations; or Billing Dept. Supervisor. Enclose a copy of the erroneous statement with your letter, plus copies of any other papers involved, and send to a street and number address, not to the box number reserved for payments. If you have a canceled check that proves payment, enclose a copy of this also—not the check itself. Here is a good letter covering a payment snarl:

#7   (Letterhead)

April 16, 19___

Supervisor
Accounting Dept.
Blank Mortgage Corp.
6832 Grant St.
Businesstown, N.Y. 00000

Re: Loan #1948322-1 and Insurance Pol. #47121841-B

Dear Sir.

January 15, 19___ we wrote your company canceling the Northern Union insurance policy #47121841-B on our building, stating that we had transferred our insurance to Walter Brown Co. We enclosed a check for the $20 substitution fee, and asked that your company send us the short rate refund due us upon cancellation of the Northern Union Policy. This notice was sent by certified mail, and we have the receipt.

Not only has no refund been made to us, but Northern Union is still billing us on the canceled policy—which they threaten to cancel. In addition, letters from your company inform us that the entire amount of our mortgage will become due immediately if our property is not covered by insurance.

We wrote you people January 25, 19___, February 3, 19___, and February 16, 19___, each time explaining the change in policies. In spite of all these efforts, apparently nothing has been done to clear up the mistakes.

We ask now that you take charge of this matter personally, and stop this harassment by your company and by Northern Union. Somewhere in your company there is a serious breakdown in communication.

We are enclosing copies of our letters to Blank Mortgage Co., a copy of our canceled check for the fee, a copy of the first page of our new insurance policy with Walter Brown Co., and also a copy of Mr. Walter Brown's letter to you people concerning the change in insurance policies.

Please let us hear from you immediately. And send us our long overdue short rate refund on the canceled Northern Union Policy #47121841-B, so that we can clear our books.

Yours very truly,

Chief Bookkeeper
Clifford Doe Co.

Encs.

Sent Certified Mail, Return Receipt Requested.

Insurance Policy Mix-ups

Making changes in insurance policy setups seems to lead to an inordinate amount of confusion. If you intend to make changes in your policies, it is usually better to deal directly with the company rather than with the local agent. One reason for this is that the agent adds another link to the chain of communication, and he himself may make an error in relaying the details of a complicated situation. As a courtesy you may send the agent a copy of your letter to the company. (See Chapter 3 on Letters Giving Instructions.)

If confusion has already developed, a careful use of numbering and tabulation can help to clarify the mess. Be sure also to address your letter to a *person* at company headquarters. Here are some useful model letters:

#8   (Letterhead)

May 10, 19___

Mr. Paul Downs, Customer Representative
Motor Insurance Co.
3642 Broad St.
Bigtown, Ill. 00000

> Truck Policies Nos.:   103479   205642
>   591836   112735

Dear Mr. Downs:

On March 14th our local agent was asked to make some changes in the four policies we carry on our trucks, but somehow errors were made. The situation is now hopelessly snarled, leaving us without insurance on one truck. This requires urgent action, as this truck must be kept out of service until the insurance is reinstated, and our business is suffering. Please give this matter your immediate attention.

Here is the story. Originally, all four of our trucks were used for delivery, and each was covered by a separate policy. On March 10, 19___, we sold the old Ford truck and replaced it with a Dodge truck. At the same time, the newer Ford truck was transferred from delivery use to use by one of our salesmen, which we understood would reduce the rate. We requested that the policy on the old Ford truck which was sold be canceled, and that a new policy be issued for the new Dodge truck. We also asked that the policy on the other (newer) Ford be modified to reflect the new use of it. As I said, there was a short circuit somewhere and instructions were not followed. (I see no point in going into details.)

This Is the Way the Policies Should Now Be Arranged:

(1) Old 1969 Ford Truck SOLD–Policy #103479 should be canceled.

(2) Newly purchased Dodge Truck, engine no. 687409358, to be covered by NEW POLICY TO BE ISSUED.

(3) 1974 Ford Pick-Up Truck, used until March 15th for deliveries exclusively, and covered by Policy #205642, was transferred for use by salesman. POLICY SHOULD BE MODIFIED to reflect this change in use, or a NEW POLICY ISSUED.

(4) 1972 Ford Truck, engine no. 8683741808, STATUS UNCHANGED. It is covered by Policy #591836, to be retained as is.

(5) 1973 Chevrolet Truck, STATUS UNCHANGED. It is covered by Policy #112735.

If you will lay out our four truck policies in front of you and put a notation on each, according to this list, I think it will be fairly easy to straighten out the mess. I urge you to please do this immediately, so that we are properly covered. Kindly airmail the corrected policies to me. In the meantime, if there are any questions, please telephone me.

Yours very truly,

Bert Sanderson, Maintenance Mgr.
Bartram Mfg., Inc.

Another Insurance Tangle Handled

#9   (Letterhead)

July 20, 19___

Mr. Gerald Barnes
Customer Relations Mgr.
Universal Insurance Co.
Street Address
Eagle Pass, S.D. 00000

Car Insur. Policy Nos.: 6989472, 704365, 9032568
Truck Policy No.: 43190746

Dear Mr. Barnes:

For some years the policies for all our motor vehicles which are insured by your company have been on Kolekt-O-Matic at Jefferson First National Bank in Bigville, with the insurance payments being taken out of our account quarterly. This proved satisfactory under old conditions. However, since we have changed our operation, dividing it into two plants at new locations, some problems developed, and so we requested that you make a change.

I wrote you on June 10, 19___, that all our motor vehicle policies were to be removed from the Kolekt-O-Matic arrangement, with all payment-due notices being sent directly to our Bookkeeping Dept. at the Culver City plant. This was done correctly in the case of the passenger cars, but for some inexplicable reason the policy on the truck was CANCELED. I was shocked to receive notice of this in today's mail. Why was this done? Can you tell me? It could not have been for non-payment, as the notice states, because the truck insurance was paid automatically by your Kolekt-O-Matic System.

It is possible, of course, that the truck bill was delayed for some unknown reason, and was presented after our account at Bigville First National was closed out. If this was the case, it seems to me inexcusable that this policy should just be automatically canceled without any prior notice to us at our new location.

I am asking you now to straighten this out in a hurry, Mr. Barnes, or your company's error will cause us great difficulty.

This Is the Way the Motor Vehicle Policies Should Now Be Handled:

	Policy #6989472 for '74 Ford Ltd., motor no. 748937245	To be billed quarterly to Culver City plant.
These Have Been Correctly Handled.	Policy #704365 for '74 Plymouth Fury, motor no. 837456193	To be billed quarterly to Culver City plant.
	Policy #9032568 for '73 Plymouth Fury, motor no. 9749684237	To be billed quarterly to Culver City plant.
This Policy Should be Reinstated.	Policy #43190746 for '73 Dodge Two-Ton Truck, motor no. 3956247818. Erroneously Canceled.	To be reinstated and billed quarterly to Culver City plant.

Please reinstate the Dodge truck insurance at once, as this truck is still in our possession. As soon as you have done so, please notify me, as well as

Miss Sharon Graham in our Bookkeeping Dept. at Culver City. If for some reason you cannot reinstate this policy, please telephone me immediately.

Yours very truly,

John N. Doe, Equipment Mgr.
Forward Mfg. Co., Inc.

If a matter like this were extremely urgent, it might have been handled first by a telephone call. In that case this letter would be a follow-up to the telephone conversation, and that fact would be mentioned at the beginning. The letter is important in any case, because it is a written record. Plan your use of tabulation and underlining carefully before you begin to write or dictate, so that it makes your requests crystal clear.

Some Repeat Letters for a Common Situation

Occasionally a first letter brings no results, and a second or third letter must be written. The following are useful models.

#10   (Letterhead)

August 15, 19___

Subscription Dept. Manager
Management World
8241 Avenue of the Americas
New York, N.Y. 00000

Re: Cancellation of Subscriptions

Dear Sir:

Last May 14th I wrote you and requested that our six subscriptions to *Management World* be canceled, because of changes in our organization, and asked for a refund to cover the remaining period of the subscriptions. It is now August and the magazines are still coming, and there has been no communication from you.

Attached hereto is a mailing label from the August issue to assist you in identifying our subscriptions. Will you please see to it that our cancellation order is put through immediately, and send us a refund check? Incidentally, I do not think that we should be charged for the July and August issues. Thank you for your prompt assistance in this matter.

Yours very truly,

Bertha K. Smith
Bookkeeping Dept.

If this letter gets no action, you might have to apply a little additional pressure, and perhaps address a different person. Here is a follow-up letter:

#11   (Letterhead)

November 15, 19____

Mr. Sedewick Perkins, Publisher
Reston Publications
8241 Avenue of the Americas
New York, N.Y. 00000

Dear Mr. Perkins:

I regret having to bring this matter to your attention, but something has to be done.

Last May 14th I wrote the Subscription Dept. Manager of *Management World* requesting that our six subscriptions to that publication be canceled, and that a refund for the remainder of the subscription period be sent us. Nothing was done, and so on August 10th I wrote again, repeating our order. Now, six months later, *Management World*—all six copies—continues to be delivered to us, and no refund has been received. In fact, there has been no communication whatsoever. This is particularly irritating because we no longer have any use for this magazine, there having been changes in our organization.

I am now appealing to you, Mr. Perkins. Can something be done about putting through our cancellation order, and sending us our refund?

Incidentally, I do not think we should be charged for any magazines sent to us after the month of June. Please let me hear from you at your earliest convenience.

Yours very truly,

Bertha K. Smith
Bookkeeping Dept.

A bit more pressure could be applied, if true, with a first paragraph like this:

As long-time subscribers to five of your magazines, our company is distressed at the treatment—or lack of treatment—we have received from *Management World.*

With the permission of your department manager, or even under his name, you might apply even more pressure, depending on the facts of the case. Instead of the first paragraph in the above letter, you might substitute something like the following:

As long-time advertisers in two of your other magazines, we are distressed at the treatment—or lack of treatment—we have received from *Management World.*

Dealing with Errors Involving Personalities

Errors involving personalities are very difficult to write about and require the utmost in tact, as some of those concerned may become angry. On the other hand, it is very important that you conceal any annoyance you may feel, if you hope to straighten out the situation and retain the cooperation and goodwill of all parties. Study the technique revealed in the following letter.

#12

Writer's address
Date

Dear Bill:

I find myself in a very embarrassing situation, and no one seems to know how it came about. I was dumbfounded when I received your plans for the committeeman's handbook. I was under the impression that Bob George had been given the task at the national convention in May. Now it seems that each of you believes that he was given the job.

I had the secretary mail me the minutes, and I find to my dismay that no decision was really made as to who was to do the handbook. This point was overlooked in the confusion. (As you remember, our speaker's plane was delayed, and I believe he arrived just at that time.)

Whatever the reason, it seems we now have two people doing the handbook—you and Bob. It occurs to me that your job is so demanding and you have done so much for the organization, that you might want to let Bob take over this project. This is the first time that he has volunteered his services, and I hate to discourage anybody from getting involved. Perhaps you would allow me to send your outline on to him, as I found it very impressive.

I cannot tell you, Bill, how sorry I am that this mess has developed, and I hope it has not caused you too much inconvenience. Please let me know immediately what you think about having Bob do the handbook, so we can work out a solution as soon as possible. I hope you know that I am grateful for the work you have done on this, and for all your efforts on behalf of the organization.

With warmest regards,

In the foregoing situation if the minutes referred to had showed that Bob George had indeed been given the job, the letter to Bill would have to be slightly different, as:

#13

1614 Home St.
Anytown, N.M. 00000
January 21, 19____

Dear Bill:

I was dumbfounded when I received your excellent plans for the committeeman's handbook. I was under the impression that Bob George had been given the task; so I had the secretary mail me the minutes of that meeting at the national convention. The minutes definitely indicate that Bob was the person given this task. However, I don't wonder that you thought otherwise, considering all the confusion there was.

Now I am on the horns of a dilemma. On the same day I received your plans, I received a complete outline from Bob, and I have to let him go ahead with this. I hope you won't mind. After all, your job is terribly demanding, and you have done so much for the organization already. In Bob's case, this is the first time he has volunteered, and you know how important it is to get as many people as possible involved in working for the organization.

Believe me, Bill, I am sorry about this misunderstanding, and I certainly hope it has not caused you too much inconvenience. I am sending your plans back to you, but I am hoping that you might send them on to Bob George. I think you have many good ideas and they would really add to the value of the handbook. Let me know what you think about this.

Thank you, my good friend, for your kind understanding in this situation—and thank you again for all the valuable work you have done in the past for our organization. I am looking forward to seeing you at the next sectional meeting, or before that, if we can manage it.

With warmest regards,

A paid employee who makes such an error as the one described above need not be handled quite so gently, but the person's feelings should still be considered, in the interest of employee morale. A letter to him might read as follows:

#14   (Letterhead)

January 21, 19___

Mr. John Jones
Peerless Co.
2029 Business St.
Bigtown, Ill. 00000

Dear John Jones:

I tried to telephone you today when the mail came, but you had already left for Springfield. I wanted to tell you to please do no further work on the manual for warehouse managers. There has been some misunderstanding. Henry Anderson, not you, was supposed to be doing this handbook; and I understand he has it well under way.

I would rather you would stick exclusively with the survey you are doing, as we need that in a hurry. Your notes on the warehouse manual were interesting, however. We'll discuss them with Anderson at the next meeting, if it's agreeable to you.

Please keep me posted on your progress with the survey.

Yours very truly,

Following Up Telephone and Telegraph Communications

Some matters are so urgent that they must be taken care of immediately by telephone or telegraph. When this is done, it is often very important to follow up with a letter repeating the details. This gives both parties a complete record of what is being discussed and what is required. In the case of a discussion over an ordinary, non-recording telephone, your letter comes as a tangible memorandum—something in hand that must be dealt with. Occasionally the letter has legal significance.

Here are examples of a few such letters. Note that they recapitulate all facts.

#15   (Letterhead)

March 4, 19___

Mr. Richard Roe, Superintendent
407 Waring Road
Worthy Contractors, Inc.
Suburbia, Colo. 00000

Re: Roofing on SQUIRES VILLAGE Unit No. 4

Dear Mr. Roe:

This is a memorandum of our telephone conversation of March 4, 19___. Our inspector, George Meredith, reported to me today that specifications in roofing for our Squires Village townhouses, Unit #4, are not being followed. He directed that roofing operations be stopped until the matter can be corrected. You agreed with this decision.

If you will refer to our original instructions, and the contract for these houses, you will note that Porter & Son MineralKing Shingles, fern green,

345#, were specified. Meredith tells us that 245# shingles are being used, and these are not up to our standard.

You agreed when this was called to your attention that any of the lower grade shingles that had been applied would be removed, and that 345# grade would be used throughout on this job.

I want to mention here that we cannot afford any delay on the Squires Village project, and we expect you not only to correct the error referred to, but also to finish the job within the required time. How you manage this is of course up to you. Please write me as soon as you can and let me know how you plan to cope with the situation. I know you will work it out to our satisfaction.

Cordially,

John Doe
Specifying Architect

It goes without saying that letters recapping telephone conversations should be absolutely accurate. Apparently Richard Roe thought that John Doe's recapitulation was less than accurate, because here is his reply, a model you might use in a similar situation.

#16

407 Waring Rd.
Suburbia, Colo. 00000
March 6, 19___

Mr. John Doe, Specifying Architect
Eminent Architects
3471 Prestige Road
Indian Rock, Colo. 00000

Dear Mr. Doe:

It probably slipped your mind, but in your memorandum of our telephone conversation of March 4, 19___ you overlooked the fact that I had said I would have to refer back to our copy of the contract on the Squires Village houses, before doing anything about the roofing matter.

I did do that immediately after talking to you, and I found that the contract for the Squires Village houses, including Unit #4, specifies the

245 lb. shingles we are using. Apparently you are so used to specifying the 345 lb. grade that no one noticed an error had been made when you had this contract typed.

Now we have a problem of a different sort. First of all, what do you want us to do, in light of the contract as it stands? Shall we continue with the 245 lb. shingles as specified in the contract? Or do you want us to substitute the 345 lb.? We cannot proceed until you let us know about this in writing.

There is also the matter of the delay. If we have to go into overtime to make your completion date, we cannot be responsible for the extra cost involved. As you know, it was your superintendent who had us interrupt the job. Again, if the 345 lb. shingles are to be substituted for work already done, and in addition we have to wait for delivery of the 345 lb. grade, there will be substantially more expense involved. We, of course, cannot absorb this extra expense either. Please consider these matters and let me have your written instructions concerning everything as soon as possible.

I want you to know I am truly sorry about this error your people typed into the contract, Mr. Doe. I had no idea that it was an error, otherwise I should have called it to your attention before proceeding. If it does turn out that there is to be extra expense involved, we shall do our utmost to keep it to a minimum. You and I might consult on this. In any case, let me know immediately what to do about the situation as it has developed.

With best regards,

Richard Roe
Worthy Contractors, Inc.

If you have to write a letter like this one from Richard Roe, concerning some actual affair of your own, you will almost certainly want to have a lawyer go over it before you send it. You should make sure that you are properly protecting yourself, and not making a bad situation worse.

Another Telephone Call Memorandum

#17

> 1791 Center St.
> Midburg, Calif. 00000
> June 5, 19___

Mr. George Brown, Service Mgr.
Foreign Car Agency
3470 S Street
Los Payasos, Calif. 00000

<u>RUSH ORDER</u>

Dear Brown:

This is a memorandum of our telephone conversation of this morning concerning wrong parts sent us. Please take every care to send us the correct parts this time, as our customer is in urgent need of his car and is getting very annoyed.

On June 2 I telephoned and ordered certain parts for a <u>220S</u>, but was sent parts for a 220SB and a 320S. As you know, I am sure, these parts do not fit the 220S, and we have been unable to complete the work for our customer. Please rush me <u>via Greyhound</u> the following correct parts.

<u>Correct Parts Needed:</u>

<u>1 220S Water Pump</u>, no. 49764974
<u>1 220S Signal Switch</u>, no. 49734782A

As soon as these correct parts are received I will return to you via Greyhound the parts that were sent me by mistake.

Thanks for your help, George—and tell those guys in the Parts Dept. to get on the ball. It doesn't do any of us any good, including Prestige Cars, when the customer is inconvenienced.

> Sincerely,
>
> J.S. Porter
> PRONTO FOREIGN CAR SERVICE

When the Customer Addresses You by Mistake

When the customer writes to you by mistake, the only point to keep in mind is to be courteous and helpful in your reply. Be careful not to seem to infer that the customer should know better. Remember that every letter you write should help to build good will for your company. Some well-worded replies follow:

#18   (Letterhead)

November 18, 19___

Mr. John Doe
705 Broad St.
Anytown, Mo. 00000

Dear Sir:

The merchandise sent us with your letter of November 14, 19___ was not manufactured by Blank & Co., and so we are returning it to you under separate cover. Our investigations indicate that these materials were probably manufactured by XYZ Co. of Dayton, Ohio. You might inquire of them.

Yours very truly,

Blank & Co.

#19   (Letterhead)

December 12, 19___

Mr. Richard Roe
912 Galahad St.
Businesstown, Ind. 00000

Dear Sir:

I have turned over your letter of December 2, 19___ to Mr. Henry Fixit in
our Adjustment Dept., and I hope that he can help you with the problem.
Any inquiries you might wish to make should be addressed to Mr. Fixit, as
he has charge of these matters.

Yours very truly,

Sales Dept.
Blank & Co.

CHAPTER 2

Letters Asking for Information

In writing for information probably the most important thing is to be clear in your own mind as to just what it is that you want to know. With this decided, plan the arrangement of your letter to make it easy for the reader to spot the item or items of information you are requesting. Tabulation is sometimes useful if a variety of points are being covered.

Requests for routine information should be as brief as possible, consistent with courtesy and clarity. If you have ever helped out in an order department, you know that a brief, clear request is a cause for rejoicing, because it saves the clerk's time. In writing for a leaflet I often use a letterhead, or even a file card with an address sticker applied to it, and keep my request to the bare essentials. The letterhead should be used if it is important to show that you are in business or have financial responsibility.

Here is an example of a "bare bones" note that serves the purpose and makes for speedy response.

#20

349 N. Main St.
Anytown, Calif. 00000
March 14, 19___

Doe, Jones and Roe, Inc., Dept. 64
792 Financial Ave.
Bigtown, Calif. 00000

Please send me a copy of your booklet on Puts and Calls, as advertised in
The Wall Street Journal on March 14th. Thank you.

(Signed) John Smith

The same time-saving form can be used for many similar requests, as "Please send me any literature you may have on lawn care products"; "Please send me any literature you may have on your new Portable Calculator #41"; "Please send me any literature you may have compiled on your new modular system."

When You Wish to Conceal Your Purpose

These "bare bones" requests have an additional usefulness on occasions when you have no intention of buying the product, yet need the information for some other purpose. At one time I was making a study of trade publications and needed information as to their circulation, character, format and editorial quality. I had no need to subscribe to any of them. If I had said this, or gone into time-consuming detail explaining my purpose, I am sure the response would not have been good. At the very least, I should have been charged for most of the copies.

With all this in mind I made the briefest possible request to the circulation department of each magazine: "Please send me a recent issue of your publication. It need not be the current issue. Any fairly recent one will do. Please let me know if there is any charge. Thank you." Back came the copies, and I was billed three dollars for only one of them!

When you want a representative or salesman to call and give you information, this same time-saving form is all that is necessary. Put the note on your business letterhead. An example:

#21

September 4, 19___

Sales Manager
Master Duplicator Corp.
1328 Main St.
Anytown, Mo. 00000

I should like to have some information about your Duplicating Machines. Please have your salesman write or telephone me for an appointment. Thank you.

Frank Smith
Publicity Mgr.

Since this is a letter to a person, you might insert "Dear Sir:" and "Yours very truly." In any case, your request will receive prompt attention.

For other situations you may wish to give more information about your needs, so that the salesman will know what to bring with him. Here is such a letter, for which a letterhead should be used:

#22

September 4, 19___

Sales Manager
Master Duplicator Corp.
1328 Main St.
Anytown, Mo. 00000

Dear Sir:

I should like to have some information about your Duplicating Machines. Please have your representative write or call me for an appointment, if you think any of your models will suit our purposes.

We must have a machine that takes <u>coated</u> <u>stock</u> and letterheads, producing high-quality copies. Speed is also important, as we are sometimes called upon to produce as many as a thousand copies within an hour. We have been using instant printing, but would prefer to do the work in our own plant. Are your machines suitable for our needs?

Yours very truly,

Frank Smith
Publicity Manager

So much for these simplest requests. Other pleas for information can require a great many more words and should be carefully organized for clarity. Some examples follow:

#23   (Letterhead)

April 14, 19___

Mr. J.R. Forward
Home Fixit Center
3047 Water St.
Jalee, Calif. 00000

Dear Mr. Forward:

At the convention last fall in Memphis you and I had quite a few discussions, and I remember your mentioning the tremendous sales you had in ATV's—All Terrain Vehicles. I was only mildly interested at the time, because this trend had not reached our area then. As a matter of fact, I had to ask you what an ATV was! Well, I know now. I must have had a dozen customers looking for them in the last month, and I wonder if you could give me some information about your experience with this line of merchandise. I don't know whether I should put in an ATV department or not. I will list the things I am particularly concerned about.

1. Can you start this in a small way, or do you have to have many different models?
2. What are your biggest selling types—4-wheel? 6? Or 8?
3. What about repairs? It seems to me that if there is no repair station in the area, I might be asking for trouble. Do you have your own repair dept.?
4. Are the ATV's still going strong in your area, or were they just a passing fad?

I know the situation here is quite different from what it is in your area, and any decision I make will have to be based on my own judgment. Still, I would be very much interested to know your opinions, and to hear about your experience with ATV's. Many thanks for any information you can give me.

With warmest regards,

Joel Nemo

Joel Nemo knows that many people hesitate to give advice, especially on a matter involving a big investment, so he makes it clear that his friend will not be blamed if things do not work out well for Nemo. He also asks definite, thoughtful questions that show he is serious. Being definite also makes sure he will get the information that he needs.

Here is a different type of letter asking for information. It is on a letterhead, of course:

#24

March 23, 19___

Mr. Nathan Green, Secretary
Chamber of Commerce
Progressive Town, Ga. 00000

Re: Plant Facilities

Dear Mr. Green:

Ours is a light manufacturing operation employing about 600 people, and we are considering moving our plant to another area if it should prove advantageous. One reason for considering Georgia is that we would be nearer the paper plant that supplies us and would save substantially on freight costs. However this is not the only consideration.

We are at present commencing a study of various locations to make sure that all necessary angles are covered, and that we achieve maximum savings in any new location. We would like your help in assessing the possibilities of Progressive Town. It will be greatly appreciated if you will give us reliable information on the following factors:

Plant—   Our needs here should not be difficult to supply. We
                   need a total of about 50,000 square feet for light

manufacturing. No heavy machinery. Plenty of daylight preferred.

Air conditioning is essential, even in paper storage areas. 10,000 square feet additional in yard space.

Location—   The closer to freight and truck terminals the better. However, must be fairly close to labor supply, with public transportation available. Some proximity to dress factories or other garment factories would be advantageous, assuring that there will be some partially trained labor available. (We expect to have to train most of our own labor in any new location.)

Labor Supply—   We should be less than candid if we did not say we hope to save on labor costs. Please let me know the average hourly rate for light-factory workers in your area. Also for highly-skilled typists. How well entrenched are unions in any nearby garment factories?

Amenities for
  Executives—   We expect to bring many of our executives with us, also some artists and writers. It will be helpful if you can tell me of housing available, also the availability of country clubs, golf courses, theaters, etc.

Taxes—   Real estate tax rates, sales taxes, special use taxes and all angles on taxation will be important to us. Please be specific here. We should of course be interested in knowing if your community is making any tax concessions to new industry.

We shall await your answer with great interest, Mr. Green. We are considering several localities, but from what we have heard we are inclined to think favorably of the Progressive Town area. In any case, if the notes you give us seem to fit in with our needs we will give them close study. Later on, of course, a delegation will investigate favored locations personally. Thank you very much for your efforts in our behalf.

Yours very truly,

Stephen Doe
Vice President

Letters Asking for Explicit Information or Instruction

#25 (Letterhead)

August 2, 19____

Plastic Adhesive & Solvent Corp.
5280 Engineer Rd.
Wayne, Ind. 00000

Att: Mr. Petersen

Dear Sirs:

We received the sample shipment of your new A-41 Plastics-to-Wood Adhesive for testing and are impressed with some of its properties. It does indeed make a smooth, seemingly permanent bond very quickly. However, we ran into some problems, and are wondering if you could give us instructions as to how to solve these. (As you know, we are not too experienced in this field.)

On many trials we find that there is always some excess adhesive that escapes in beads at the edges. When the solvent is used to remove these it damages the edges of the plastic sheet and also changes the color of the wood in spots. Is there a foolproof method for removing these beads?

Another problem we have had is with the very quickness of the bond, which is advantageous in other ways. We find that when the plastic layer is applied it cannot be moved one iota, and the edges then have to be ground or sanded to correct the error. This is entirely too time-consuming. Have you a solution to this problem of accurately placing the plastic layer every time?

Please let us hear from you at your earliest convenience. We must decide soon on whether or not we will use your adhesive, as supplies of the old type are running low. Also it will make considerable difference in our operation and in our scheduling.

Yours very truly,

James Venture, Supt.
Laminating Division

#26   (Letterhead)

March 22, 19___

Mr. Joel Newby, Sales Dept.
Maintenance Supplies Co.
7482 Main St.
Anytown, N.J. 00000

Dear Mr. Newby:

We have been pleased with the durability and the appearance your A47
Quick Wax gives to our asphalt tile hallways, but we have run into a
problem with it. Now that it has been in use for about two months we find
a wax film is riding up the walls of the hallways. This is unsightly and
difficult to remove. Any time we save in application of the wax is being
wasted now in trying to keep these walls clean.

Have you had complaints about this problem from others? And is there a
solution? Please let me have your answer as soon as possible. Thank you.

James Roe, Maintenance Mgr.
County Operations Center

In the above letter the questioner makes sure of getting a
speedy answer by addressing his letter to the salesman, and also by
indicating that he is sold on the product except for its one apparent
fault. The salesman will be anxious to keep him sold, and so he will
hasten to send him the information requested.

Some Requests for Additional Information

The next letter is addressed to a merchandiser of printed
business forms, and was sent in reply to a sales letter.

#27 (Letterhead)

April 27, 19___

Form Systems, Inc.
3247 Busy Street
Metropolis, N.Y. 00000

Dear Sirs:

I have just read your letter concerning the savings in time that can be accomplished in hospitals by the use of your coordinated business forms. The concept is interesting; however, I do not believe the systems especially designed for hospitals would be applicable to the operation of a convalescent home.

If you have a coordinated plan especially designed for our type of operation, I should be interested in hearing about it. You might send me a sample set of such forms. I can tell from this whether it would be worth your time or mine for you to come out here. Thank you.

Yours very truly,

Manager
Sunnydale Rest Home

In the following letter in response to a "Business Opportunities" ad, the writer makes it clear that he is a good prospect, thus assuring an answer to his very definite query.

#28 (Letterhead)

June 23, 19___

Postal Machine Co.
Modern Industrial Park
Businesstown, Calif. 00000

Dear Sirs:

Since we operate many vending machine routes, we are interested in obtaining information concerning the new postage vending machines you advertise in today's *Businesstown News.*

The drawback to most postage vending machines in our view is the amount of time required to refill them—manually sorting the stamps and placing them in the little folders. This makes them completely profitless from any practical standpoint.

Our first question is this: Do the new machines involve the same time-consuming feature?

We should also like to know what the $5,500 investment covers. Does it purchase the machines, or only the route?

A prompt reply will be appreciated.

Yours very truly,

John Doe, Mgr.
Machine Div.

Here are two letters asking for additional information about a prospective employee. In both cases the writer is encouraging, but is careful not to promise employment when this information is furnished. Both letters are on letterheads.

#29

October 11, 19____

Mr. Harold Smith
1400 Main St.
Friendlytown, Ohio 00000

Dear Hal:

I have your note of last week asking about employment for your young friend, Hubert Worthy. As you know, things have been slow in our field, but one opening has recently occurred in the work force. We need an assistant to the warehouse manager.

The person hired need not be experienced. The manager will train him. However, he must have aptitude for detail and have an interest in machines and machine parts.

You didn't tell me much about Hubert. Perhaps it would be a good idea to have him write me as soon as he can, and include a resume.

I know this matter is important to you, Hal, and I will certainly help if it is at all possible.

With warmest personal regards to you and Rose,

(Signed) Bob

#30   (Letterhead)

March 10, 19____

Mr. Richard Roe
1722 Front St.
Anytown, S.C. 00000

Dear Sir:

We were impressed with your letter in answer to our advertisement, but should like to have a little more information before asking you to make the trip here for an interview. If you will be kind enough to answer these few questions it will be most helpful.

We note that your sales experience is extensive, but we wonder if you have had any actual experience with paper products. Have you any contacts that would be valuable in this field?

The other questions are routine but necessary to our assessment.

1. How long have you been with your present employer?
2. Would you be willing to relocate in Ohio or New Mexico? If so, which would you prefer? (Moving expenses will be paid.)
3. What is your marital status?
4. May we contact your present employer?

Please let us have your reply at your earliest convenience, and we will notify you of our decision promptly.

Sincerely,

Herbert R. Jones
Sales Manager

Letters Requesting Prices

Letters asking for prices on a given item or a standard line of goods can be quite brief. Those that require an estimate on work or the manufacture of something must often be quite lengthy, and they should be checked to make sure every detail has been covered. Taking care with the first letter often saves extensive correspondence and costly errors. The examples given are both on letterheads.

#31

September 3, 19___

Mr. John Smith, Sales Manager
Volume Printing Co.
34 West St.
Bigtown, Mich. 00000

Dear Sir:

Enclosed is a copy of our January Home Sale catalog of this year. We should like to have an estimate from your company on the printing of the next one, if you are equipped to do the complete job. This would include collating and binding; but we would furnish camera-ready copy.

As you will note, the enclosed catalog was printed in two colors. We should like to have estimates on a similar two-color job; but we should also like to have your prices for a full color job—you to do the color-separation in both cases.

Please give us your estimates on 25,000 copies; 50,000 copies; and 100,000 copies.

Yours very truly,

Advertising Manager

#32

January 17, 19___

Sales Manager
General Jar & Bottle Corp.
Commercial City, N.J. 00000

Re: Cosmetic Jars

Dear Sir:

We are trying to locate a source for plastic cosmetic jars for a new product that is being developed. At present we require only about 5 gross for our salesmen, but we expect to have greatly expanded requirements in the near future.

We need 2½ or 3 oz. jars with screw-on lids, white or pastel, which are resistent to grease, perfume, and fruit acids. We should like to have them imprinted in gold, but could use a label if imprinting is impractical.

Please quote us prices on 1,000 jars, 10,000 jars, and 100,000 jars—both plain and imprinted. Please give complete description with your price quotes; or better yet, send samples. Thank you.

Very truly yours,

Oscar W. Jones, Vice Pres.

Asking Clarification of Price List

#33   (Letterhead)

March 11, 19___

Giftwares Importer
1440 Broadway
Metropolis, N.Y. 00000

Dear Sirs:

We are interested in a number of the giftwares shown in the April catalog you sent us recently, but there is confusion about prices on two of the items. Would you please clarify the price listing on these?

(1) #746 Italian Marble Birds. The 3" size is listed at $4 each, and the 6" size at $2 each. Is this correct?

(2) #2137 Ormolu Baskets, 4", are listed simply at $72. We assume this is not the item price. What quantity is priced at $72?

In addition to clarification of the listing on the above items, we should like to know quantity prices. Do you give a standard discount on 1-gross orders? 10-gross orders? If not, please quote us 1-gross and 10-gross prices on #1940, #2137, and #3290. Ours is now a six-store operation and we may wish to order in quantity.

A reply by return mail will be appreciated.

Yours very truly,

Jason Roe
EXOTIQUE GIFTS, INC.

CHAPTER 3

Model Letters Giving Instructions

In writing instructions to someone there are two important things to keep in mind. The first, making your instructions clear and orderly, is obvious. The second thing is embodied in the style and approach of your letter. Here you want to be careful to avoid a condescending manner, or anything that might be construed as insulting. Do not say, "I thought my instructions were perfectly clear, " or "I'll try to make it simpler," or any such thing. Just answer the questions and repeat and amplify the instructions as necessary. If anything, you might want to use an apologetic phrase on occasion. To someone you do not know too well you might say, "I am probably going into more detail than necessary, but I don't know how familiar you are with the process." Or again, "I will just include everything, and you can skip what you already know."

The answers to two letters in the previous chapter (#25 and #26) are good examples of diplomacy in furnishing information. In both cases the questioner had shown himself inexperienced. In the case of the maintenance manager and the floor wax problem the salesman probably said to himself, "Ye gods! Here's a guy in charge of maintenance and he doesn't know this elementary thing!" Be that as it may, the salesman's job is to sell his products, not insult his customers, and so he tactfully presents the information required.

#34   (Letterhead)

March 25, 19____

Mr. James Roe, Maintenance Mgr.
County Operations Center
Middleburg, Tex. 00000

Dear Mr. Roe:

Thank you for giving me the opportunity to explain the properties of our very durable A47 Quick Wax. When I demonstrated the A47 I should have told you that the very best waxes have a tendency to "flow" on asphalt tile, especially under heavy traffic. This is what is causing your problem of the wax creeping up the wall, and it is very easily remedied.

(1) The first application of the wax should be made from the center of the hallway and should be very much thinned out as it approaches walls. In addition, this first coat should not go right to the wall, but should be feathered off four to six inches away from the wall. (You may think this will be noticeable, but it will not be, I assure you.)

(2) The second application of A47, and all later applications, should be finished off at least one foot away from any wall. The reason for this is that under the friction of foot traffic the more durable waxes do not wear out, but work out imperceptibly or "flow" toward the edges. Even though the wax is never applied close to the walls, it eventually gets to them.

After a month or so of applying the wax the floor-care man should keep a close eye out for the effects of this movement. If he finds the wax approaching the walls, he should carefully clean a two-foot strip along the edges with our A47X Stripper, rinsing with a damp mop wrung out of ammonia water. He can then proceed with the regular waxing. (Because A47 is self-cleaning, there is no need to strip or wash the center area.)

Incidentally, since our A47 Quick Wax is exceptionally durable, you should caution your man to apply it sparingly and let it dry thoroughly before polishing. An occasional buffing will keep the floors bright for an unusually long time, without the application of more wax. This is a definite economy feature of A47. With the situation you have run into it might be a good idea to apply no more wax at all after cleaning the side strips, until the wax "flow" is greatly slowed down.

Again, thank you, Mr. Roe, for allowing me to explain the properties of our super-durable A47 Quick Wax. It is the very durability of it that has caused some of the trouble—you need less than with other waxes. I am sure you will have no further problems, but if a question should come up, please don't hesitate to contact me.

Yours very truly,

Joel Newby
Maintenance Supplies Co.

Here is the answer to the letter asking for additional information on the plastic-to-wood adhesive:

#35
Letterhead

August 7, 19___

Mr. James Venture, Supt.
Laminating Division
Handy Module Co.
Busytown, O. 00000

Re: Queries Regarding A41 Adhesive

Dear Mr. Venture:

I am glad that you wrote me about the problems you have encountered, because we want you to get the full benefit of any of our products that you use. Luckily some rather simple solutions have been worked out.

Answer to Question 1: For easy removal of beads, the edge of the wood should be prepared prior to placing of plastic layer. Apply our special masking tape to the wood edge BEFORE the adhesive-coated plastic is laid on the wood. Almost immediately, this tape can be stripped off, taking beads or runs with it. (Of course, when your men become experienced they will find just the correct amount of adhesive to apply, and the use of the tape will become unnecessary.)

Answer to Question 2: Accurately placing the plastic layer on the wood becomes easy if guide-blocks are used. Temporarily nail two uniform wood blocks to each edge of the wood top, near each corner. (Ready-formed steel guide blocks could also be used.) With the blocks in place, the plastic layer can be slid down between them to a perfect landing. The blocks can then be easily removed to use again. Plug up nail holes with any filler.

Because I know how anxious you are to get on with your experimental run, I am mailing you under separate cover a sample roll of the A41 Special Masking Tape. I am sure you will find it a great time saver.

If you run into any further problems with A41, Mr. Venture—but I do not think you will—please write me again. Actually, when your workmen get used to it, they will find this improved adhesive a great time-saver, and thus a money-saver.

With very best regards,

Joel Newby, Sales Dept.

Enc.

The enclosure, which Newby did not mention, was a sales leaflet and an order form for more adhesive and tape. Note that his letter does quite a selling job for the product as well as explaining its use.

The following letter from an advertising agency to an out-of-town client gives very explicit instructions, but it starts out with an enthusiastic bit of selling.

#36   **(Letterhead)**

September 20, 19___

Mr. Clark Jones, Manager
The Smart Shop
Middletown, Ark. 00000

Dear Mr. Jones:

Well, we have everything set for a really great series of Pre-Christmas promotions. I think you can look forward to a substantial increase in business. I went over all the finished pieces in series today and I was impressed, as I am sure you will be, with the samples I am enclosing.

To make sure there is no hitch, the letter and the two mailing pieces have been packed in three separate boxes and each box color-keyed, so that it need not be opened until you are ready to do the addressing and mailing. As we agreed, all pieces should be mailed from your own city to emphasize the local flavor of the campaign. I would suggest that you plan to mail each promotion piece no less than one week previous to the scheduled event. With this in mind you can prepare to have the addressing done well ahead of time. (Your indicia was imprinted, of course.)

Color-Keying

The box for each date is strapped with a different-colored tape. As an additional precaution, the envelopes within a box are marked with a colored dot to match the color key tape.

Blue to be Mailed October 30th
Yellow to be Mailed November 10th
Green to Mailed November 25th

To aid in informing your people of the mailing plan I have had a quantity of small signs printed up giving the color keys opposite the dates. I hope these will be helpful. I suggest you post them in any area where a reminder might be needed.

I know you are coming into a hectic merchandise period now, Mr. Jones, but when you have a little free time don't forget that we should like to estimate on any post-Christmas events you may be considering. In the meantime, I want to wish you a very happy Pre-Christmas! (I'll be down in person to bring my good wishes at Christmas time.)

Sincerely,

Richard Roe

Encs.

Sometimes letters recommending a product or a process must include a certain amount of instruction. In writing such letters be careful to hedge your recommendations and protect yourself against any damage that might be caused by following your suggestions. Here is a good letter written from one friend to another.

#37 (Letterhead)

February 4, 19___

Mr. William Smith, Vice Pres.
Precise Instruments, Inc.
Industrialville, Conn. 00000

Dear Bill,

I was sorry to hear you have had so much trouble with breakage and shock damage in the shipping of your new optical scanner. Such troubles can really cut into profit.

I am not sure it will serve your purpose, but you might experiment with foam-spray packaging. We have had great success with it. I suggest you contact several companies that make the stuff and have them demonstrate its use. We have been using the Stellar Age product. They furnish a small compact system that includes everything needed, including the spray gun and hoses.

There are different ways of using the foam, but this is the way we use it in packing our X390 balance wheels. We tape together a good sized collapsible paper carton and spray a bed of the plastic foam in the bottom. On top of this we place the wheel, which has been encased in a polyethylene bag, with all air expressed.

The next step is to place pegs in the bed surrounding the wheel. The pegs are of uniform size and extend 5 inches above the foam bed. (Five inches is half the height of the wheel package.)

On top of the pegs a corrugated board is placed. This has a cutout in the middle that exactly fits the wheel package, and it has another hole in it that just fits the spray gun nozzle. The operator now fills the space under the cardboard layer with foam. Next he sprays on top of the cardboard layer, after taping over the nozzle aperture, completely covering the plastic package and filling the box.

The foam-spray firms up instantly, and the resulting package is about as shockproof as anything you could imagine. The cardboard layer in the center makes it easy to remove the foam block when the merchandise is being unpacked.

Ingenious, eh what? As I say, this packing method works great for us on these expensive individual items. Let me know what you think about it.

Cordially,

(Signed)   John

Instructions to salesmen, and to most other employees, will sit better if the reasoning behind them is explained. The following letter is a good example.

#38 (Letterhead)

November 14, 19___

Mr. Henry White
Commercial Hotel
Bigtown, Tenn. 00000

Dear Representative: (Or the name may be filled in.)

The tremendous reception given our new line of silent calculators and auditing machines in the last six months has made it necessary to realign territories in some degree. As you know, the phenomenal number of sales has made it impossible for representatives to give proper service to all past customers. Time that can be devoted to making new contacts has also been greatly reduced, cutting into your opportunities for added income. Success has become a problem!

The management board and I have wrestled with this pleasant but very real problem and decided that a realignment of territories is the only solution. How to make this realignment fair to everyone then had to be worked out.

This Is the Plan We Came Up With

Every senior salesman's old territory will be greatly reduced, sometimes eliminated, through a new pattern of territories. At the same time a large new area will be added to give an opportunity for NEW SALES.

How Commissions Will Work Out

(1) You will continue to collect commissions on all past sales until the accounts are cleared on all items you sold.

(2) You will of course be entitled to full commission on new sales.

(3) You will service any of the former salesman's accounts that are now included in your realigned territory, but you will not collect commissions on these until new sales are made to these customers at some time in the future. This rule applies to everyone equally—all salesman.

YOUR NEW TERRITORY
Beginning February 1, 19___

Instructions to: Mr. Henry White

Beginning February 1 next year you will operate out of our new office in Richmond, Virginia. Please see attached map for actual area included. If there are any questions, please contact me immediately.

In closing I want to congratulate you on your excellent record in the recent past, and to wish you all good luck in the future. I believe everyone will be much happier with the new arrangement, and with the expanded territories.

Sincerely,

William Smith, Sales Mgr.

Some instruction letters are much simpler. Here is one written to a rural customer by a washing machine manufacturer.

#39   (Letterhead)

March 3, 19___

Mrs. John Doe
R.F.D. Route 147
Littleville, N.Y. 00000

Dear Mrs. Doe,

It is unfortunate that you lost your instruction manual for the Magna Washer, because the problem you encountered is covered on Page 32, and is something that could have been taken care of in a moment. A new manual is being sent to you under separate cover, so that you will be saved any such difficulty in the future.

When your washer stops suddenly in the middle of a run it is almost always an indication that there is an unbalanced load. (The unbalancing triggers a safety mechanism to prevent damage to the washer.) When this happens, follow these simple steps:

1. Reach in and rearrange the garments and other items in the tub so as to distribute weight evenly. Close tub lid.
2. Pull down the lower front apron of the washer. On the extreme left, at the lower corner, you will see a Red Button. Press this. (It releases and resets the safety mechanism.)
3. Pull out the standard "Wash" button at upper right of washer. The machine will now resume the wash cycle or spin cycle at the point where it was stopped by the safety mechanism

We are so sorry you had this difficulty, Mrs. Doe, and hope now that everything will be fine. We believe our Magna Washer is a superior home appliance, and it should serve you for years with the minimum of care. Thank you for writing us.

> John R. Smith
> CUSTOMER SERVICE DEPT.

In-house memoranda giving instructions are written in much the same way. Tabulation and the numbering of succeeding steps in the directions do much to give clarity. Note how these are used in the following notice to salespeople in a store. (These instructions were handed out to individuals at a meeting.)

#40

June 11, 19___

To All Salespeople:

HOW TO USE THE NEW SALESCHECK

Please note that the new salescheck, as shown in the illustration, has three parts rather than four. This should save time for you. However, it is important that all parts be filled in properly, and that you distribute the parts correctly. Saleschecks will still be made out in triplicate, so make sure that both carbons are in place before you begin to write.

ADDRESS LABEL: Fill this in for all sales except Paid-Take, for which a cash register receipt is given. Always fill in the address label first, in the following order:

1. For all sales clearly check one of the four small boxes at upper left, indicating whether the sale is Paid, Charge, C.O.D., or Will Call.
2. For a Charge-Take purchase, clearly check the box at upper right which is marked TAKE. On a Charge-Take you need not fill in anything else on the address label.
3. For Charge-Send, C.O.D., or Will Call sales, PRINT the customer's name and address as indicated on address label. Fill in zip code.

BODY OF CHECK: Fill this in for all sales except Paid-Take, for which a cash register receipt is given.

4. Check small boxes at top of check, just as for the address label.

5. Fill in department number and your number in the boxes marked for this purpose. (You must do this in order to get credit for the sale.)

6. Fill in quantity and name of each item and unit price, just as you are accustomed to. Put prices in right hand column, add them up and add tax, just as we do now.

BOTTOM VOUCHER: Carefully check boxes at top as you did on the other two parts of the salescheck. Write in the Total Amount of purchase, including tax.

WHAT TO DO WITH THE PARTS

Carefully go over your work to make sure you have filled in all the information required, then tear out the Original and the Duplicate. (The tissue triplicate remains in your book until you place it in your tally at night.) Place carbon between original and duplicate and insert in cash register with customer's charge plate as we have always done. Punch price and your number.

ADDRESS LABEL: For Charge-Take sales only, when address is not filled in: Place Original and Duplicate Address Labels on "Take" spindle.

For all other sales for which a salescheck is used, place Original and Duplicate of Address Label with the merchandise. (Pin on when possible.)

BODY OF CHECK: The Original goes on the spindle marked Auditing Dept.

For Charge-Take sales, when you wrap the merchandise, place duplicate in bag with the merchandise.

For all sales that require the merchandise to go to the wrapper, place duplicate with merchandise.

BOTTOM VOUCHER: Original goes into the customer's hand, whenever a salescheck is used.

Duplicate voucher goes to the wrapper with the merchandise, except in the case of Take sales. For Take sales that you wrap, the bottom voucher goes on the "Take" spindle. (No salescheck parts are ever thrown away.)

Note: It is very important that all parts of the salescheck be sent to the proper place or person, so that all departments concerned will get the information they need. If you are in doubt about any step in this process, please refer to this notice, or ask your supervisor for instruction.

CHAPTER 4

Some Difficult Asking Letters
Made Easy–22 Model Letters

"I hate to ask him, but I've got to." What a familiar phrase this is! Nearly everybody does a bit of writhing before he can bring himself to write an *asking* letter. He feels that he is putting himself in the position of an inferior. Worse yet, he secretly fears being degraded by a refusal.

Banish such thoughts summarily if you would write such a letter successfully. If you do not, your letter may become obsequious, or go to the opposite pole and carry an undercurrent of defeating resentment. Remind yourself that everyone in the world has to ask for something sometime, including the man you are writing to! Better yet, dwell on the truth that nearly everyone *likes* to be asked for help or to give help. Sometimes an excellent way to create a friendly feeling toward yourself is to give the other fellow a chance to do you a favor.

Here are some gracefully-worded asking letters that should bring the desired results. Choose one that suits your purpose, or combine the phrasing of a couple of them in composing your own request.

Asking a Favor

#41 (Letterhead)

May 3, 19___

Mr. Robert Brown
912 Broad St.
Anytown, Mass. 00000

Dear Mr. Brown,

I know that I told you you could have two weeks to finish the artwork for our Pre-School Catalog, but I now find I am not going to be able to allow you that much time. The printer tells us he is so rushed that he must have all material, camera-ready, by May 20th. Deducting the minimum of six days that it will take our Production Dept. to assemble the stuff, that leaves just eleven days for you to finish the art and get it to us.

Can you do it in this time? And will you, as a favor?

You know I like the character of your work, and I like to have the same feel, the same atmosphere throughout the circular. On the other hand, if I am pressing you too hard and you absolutely cannot finish the drawings in the shortened time, I suppose I will have to compromise. You could rush some of the photos back to me.

What do you say? Can you do the job for me on this shortened schedule? I know I needn't tell you how much I will appreciate it. Please let me have your answer by return mail.

Sincerely,

Brad Jones, Adv. Mgr.

#42   (Letterhead)

March 30, 19___

Mr. Robert S. Smith
Southwest Industries
1211 Fifth Street
San Diego, Ca. 00000

Dear Bob,

I wonder if I could ask a favor of you? A very good friend and customer of mine, Ralph Jones of Modern Instruments, is going to be vacationing in San Diego for two weeks, beginning May 12th. He is a complete stranger in your city and will be by himself. When he mentioned this, of course I had to go and say that I knew somebody there. Is it all right with you if I have him call you? And could you spare the time to show him around a bit?

I realize I should have asked you this before I even mentioned your name, but what's done is done. On the other hand I think you would enjoy Ralph's company. He's a fisherman and a low-eighties golfer, and quite a witty fellow. He is quality control engineer at Modern.

What do you say? Shall I give Ralph a letter of introduction? Any little thing you can do to make his stay more enjoyable will be greatly appreciated by me. And of course I will be delighted to return the favor at any time you might want me to.

Please say hello to Marian and the children for me. I wish I were coming with Jones, but I am swamped with work at this season.

With warmest regards,

(Signed)   John

#43   (Letterhead)

February 10, 19___

Mr. Jacob Green, President
Success Stores, Inc.
910 Broadway
Big City, Ill. 00000

Dear Jake:

As you know, I have a small department store in this city doing a volume
of three million, which is only fair for the size of the store and the
location. After listening to your talk last year about the importance of
increasing the size of a retail operation in order to secure price advantages
and sell competitively, I have made a real effort to open branch stores.

I did take on one branch store about six months ago, and it is doing fairly
well, but I have had difficulty locating another. Finally there is one
available, but I have some doubts about it, chiefly because of the location.
It is well situated in a busy shopping center with plenty of parking space
and plenty of traffic, but the shopping center is only about ten miles from
the main store.

My staff has been no help at all on making this decision. They are divided,
right down the middle. I am now wondering if I could ask a tremendous
favor of you. Could you possibly get down here for a few days, look over
the situation, and give me your opinion?

I would want you to stay with Janice and me. You could make it a little
vacation. We have a tennis court, and there are two good golf courses
nearby. There's the lake, too, if you like boating or fishing. What do you
say? Perhaps Mrs. Green would like to come along, and she would be most
welcome.

Let me add that I would certainly not hold you responsible for any
decision I might finally make on the second branch store. I just feel that I
need the advice of a really successful, more experienced operator in this
field. May Janice and I roll out the red carpet?

With very best regards,

(Signed)   Harry

Harry Roe, President

When he wrote the above letter Harry Roe was tempted to hoodwink Jake Green by just inviting him as a house guest, then maneuvering him into giving an opinion. He thought better of it and decided to be direct. Jake Green would probably have seen through any scheming and resented it.

Asking for Additional Help, for More Cooperation

#44   (Letterhead)

January 10, 19___

Mr. John White, Gen. Mgr.
Expanding Industry, Inc.
3447 Factory St.
Big City, Ohio 00000

Dear Mr. White:

As you know, sir, the overall volume of our business has increased 50% within the last few months. This is good for us all; however, it is creating problems in the shipping division here. We have taken up every bit of slack in our system and have instituted time-saving methods wherever we could, but we are still falling behind on the delivery schedule.

I believe we have gotten to the point where we simply must add at least four persons to our crew here. Delays on outgoing orders, if they get much worse may actually hurt us with our customers, and undo some of the benefits of the increased volume of business. At the same time our present staff is becoming disgruntled with the constant overload, and we may lose some of our best people.

In view of this situation, I ask your permission, sir, to hire at least four new crew members. I know this is beyond our present budget, but is there perhaps a contingency fund that would provide this help? I believe the additional staff would be for the good of the business, now and in the long run. May I please hear from you immediately?

Respectfully,

James Bradford

#45   (Letterhead)

January 12, 19___

Mr. James Bradford
Shipping Dept. Mgr.
Expanding Industry, Inc.
2991 Fifth St.
Industrial Park, Ohio 00000

Dear Bradford:

I can well understand some of the problems you are running into with the increased volume of deliveries, but it is a problem we are going to have to solve within our present scope. As an important member of management, you are being asked to share management's dilemma at this point in our growth. Part of this will be persuading your people to really buckle down and put out at this stage of the game so that we can all share in the future benefits of expansion.

Here is the situation, but I want these details to be kept absolutely confidential. We consider it imperative for some months that we stay within the current budget. It is a matter of interest rates. We could borrow against the new business, but we do not wish to at today's high rates, especially when lower rates are being forecast by all indicators.

I know this is scant comfort, but it is something we have to live with, and I know I can count on you for full cooperation. To tide you over this tough spot I am tightening up our own operation, and next week I will send you two people from our office staff. They are Richard Roe and John Doe, two strong and bright young fellows that you can easily train. Their personnel records and transfers are being sent to you immediately under separate cover.

Cordially,

John White, Gen. Mgr.

Asking for More Time

When you have agreed to do something or to make a delivery by a certain date it is embarrassing to have to ask for more time, but it is most important that you do so. Face the issue and explain clearly what the situation is, and the person you are dealing with will be grateful to you. You give him the opportunity to adjust to the altered schedule. Note how it is done in these model letters:

#46   (Letterhead)

October 15, 19___

Mr. Alan Johnson, Systems Engineer
Three-Valley Power Complex
Wayside, Ala. 00000

Re: Disc Memory System Study

Dear Mr. Johnson:

The more I get into the Disc Memory System study for use in your Three-Valley Complex the more positive I become that it will give you a much smoother operation, with far fewer breakdowns, thus saving your company a great deal of money. I had hoped to get all details into your hands by November 30th, as we discussed, but I am finding that the drawing of the plans is going to take a little more time than I had anticipated. (As you pointed out, yours is an intricate operation.)

It now seems that January 3 of next year would be a more realistic date for the presentation to your management—you and I can go over the complete setup by December 15th. I hope that you will not be greatly inconvenienced by this delay, but I did want to let you know about it well ahead of time so that you can plan accordingly. I am sure you will agree with me that it is better to have every detail taken care of, rather than to have loose ends that may invite needless misunderstandings. Of course, if it is absolutely necessary, I could make a quite convincing presentation, even at the present stage of the plans, but Valley Three would not be shown as completely integrated.

Please let me know your opinion as to which route we should go. I am hoping, of course, that the January 3rd target date will be acceptable. Thank you for your consideration and understanding.

With best personal regards,

Joseph Doe, Vice Pres.
DISC MEMORY SYSTEMS CO.

Note that in the above letter the writer introduces his request for more time with a restatement of his powerful selling points. In effect, the writer is saying that whatever he is offering is worth waiting for. He is also giving the other man a sales talk to present to his superiors when he must prepare for the change in dates.

#47

3413 Second St.
Neartown, Wash. 00000
May 29, 19___

Mr. Henry Roe
Leading Art Agency
Bigtown, Wash. 00000

Dear Hank:

The cut glass merchandise you sent me is far more ornate than I had visualized, and it is a hell of a thing to do justice in the rendering. I have done quite a few of the pieces in pen and ink and they look great; however, I am afraid I am going to have to ask for two more days to complete them all. I hope this won't mess up your schedule too badly, but I don't think anyone could do these pieces any faster. Please telephone me immediately if you can't grant me this extra time, and we will see what we can work out. In the meantime, I'll keep everlastingly at it.

Best—

Dick

#48   (Letterhead)

April 7, 19___

Mr. I.J. Kay
Diversified Industries
Westville, Calif. 00000

Dear Mr. Kay:

I know that I promised you a decision on the Fairfield matter by the end of this week, but I still cannot quite make up my mind. I should like to do a little more research, and I also want to confer with Mr. Carl Jennings. Unfortunately, I will not be able to see Jennings until the end of next week, as he has been called away unexpectedly. If it is at all possible, I am hoping that you will be able to grant me two more weeks for my studies. What do you say? Can you fit this in with your plans?

With very best regards,

RICHARD ROE

Asking for Reconsideration of a Decision

#49   (Letterhead)

September 5, 19___

Mr. John Jones, Purchasing Agent
Eastern Manufactures, Inc.
Bigtown, N.J.

Dear Mr. Jones:

After talking to you yesterday it occurred to me that I had not emphasized enough the actual money savings achieved by having a copier that will work with any kind of paper—does not require special coated stock. Our studies show that the extra cost of the special paper some machines require amounts to a great deal in a few years—enough to actually pay the purchase price of our Magic Copy machine.

I am enclosing a sheet showing comparative costs of paper used by various machines, so that you can go over them and check them against your own experience. When you look at these figures, please note that this material is printed on an ordinary letterhead of medium quality—uncoated. This is an example of routine work done on the Magic Copy, yet is so clear and clean it could be used for a mailing piece. It is far clearer than most copies on special coated stock coming from other machines.

I am sorry that I did not bring out this important cost-saving factor sufficiently in our last talk, but now that I have given some hard figures I am hoping you may reconsider your decision. If you would like a demonstration on your own letterhead or on any paper at all, I will be happy to bring the Magic Copy to your place at any time convenient to you. You can reach me at 232-9740, Extension 21.

With very best regards,

(Signature)
for MAGIC COPY

Encl.

There is an important point involved in the phrasing of the above letter. Some letter writers might automatically say, "I don't think you really understood what savings you could make by using uncoated paper," or "I do not think you realized how much you could save by using the Magic Copy and uncoated paper." Such approaches would turn the reader off immediately, because they unwittingly attack his intelligence. A gesture of irritation would land the letter in the waste basket.

Whether he actually was to blame or not, the writer of the above letter puts the blame on himself as though he were not a good salesman. He thus gives himself a chance to bear down heavily on an important selling point. He gains a sympathetic reading, and just may persuade the customer to reconsider his turndown.

Asking for a Contribution

#50   (Letterhead or In-House Memo)

May 2, 19___

Mrs. Rosemarie Smith, Supervisor
Billing Dept.
Modern Stores, Inc.
3442 West St.
Anytown, Kansas 00000

Dear Mrs. Smith:

We don't know whether you have heard the news or not, but Sally Jones, Head of Stock in the Junior Apparel Division, who has been with Modern Stores for nine years, is going to be married next June 23rd. Those of us who work with her thought it would be fun to have a luncheon party for her in a couple of weeks and present her with a nice gift. While we were planning this we realized that many people in other departments have become friends of Sally's over the years, and might want to join us.

If you would like to be in on the celebration, please let me know by May 10th. We are asking a contribution of $3.00 for the luncheon, which will be held at the Bonton here—plus whatever you wish to contribute toward the gift.

We hope to see you at the Bonton. We will send all details, the date and the time later. Have you any suggestions about the gift? We thought some handsome luggage would be a good choice.

(Signed)   Adele May, Lingerie

The main point to note in the above request for a contribution is the fact that Adele May mentions the gift that is being considered. Many persons are very irritated when they are asked to contribute to something, and yet are not let in on the plans.

Asking Someone to Share Responsibility

#51   (Letterhead)

                                            April 7, 19___

Mr. Clark Roe, Vice Pres.
Aero Co.
9000 Fire Drive
Hub City, Ill. 00000

    Re: 16-324792-996 Wafer Pack

Dear Mr. Roe:

I hesitate to trouble you with this, but I feel that I must have your opinion on a matter of this importance before I make a directive. Although the entire lot of 200 of the above Wafer Packs had been passed by Mo. Testing, our Vidicon exam showed many pinholes in the solder joining the layers. Microscopic and other tests confirmed this finding. No such tests are required by MIL STD covering this part; however, our Quality Control rejected the entire lot of 200 and returned it to Triangle. I agreed with this decision, although I was not happy with it. It sets our program back by at least eight months.

Today something else has come up in regard to the Wafer Pack, and that is the point on which I should like your advice. Triangle reluctantly took back the parts, but retested them and confirmed our findings. Now, however, Triangle asks to be allowed to correct the faulty seals by running the entire lot of Wafer Packs through the sealing process for a second time. This sounds fine, except that in my opinion the resealing process may damage internal bonds in the Wafer Packs, and there is no completely reliable test for this. Defects not discernible now may show up in later operation.

I would not hesitate to reject the proposal, except, as I have said, our program will be delayed at least eight months if we must wait for construction of new Wafer Packs. What do you think we should do? I shall greatly appreciate your considered opinion on this.

                Yours very truly,

                A.B. Cee, Parts Engineering

Asking About a Gift Never Acknowledged

#52   (Letterhead)

January 23, 19____

Mr. Richard Roe
Roe Company
Main St.
Anytown, Nev. 00000

Dear Roe:

I know you have been terrifically busy these last few weeks, but I just
wanted to check with you to make sure a package arrived that was mailed
to you last November 15th. It contained a gift to celebrate your grand
opening—a green morocco desk set. The package was insured, and if you
never got it, I want to have the post office put a tracer on it. When you
have a minute, please drop me a line.

With all good wishes for your success,

(Signed)   Henry Jones

The reason for describing the gift in the above note is that
donor's cards sometimes get separated from the items sent on some
gift occasion, and the recipient does not know whom to thank. If he
has merely been careless about his thank you's, this suggests an
excuse the recipient can use to save mutual embarrassment.

Asking About Receipt of a Letter Not Answered

#53   (Letterhead)

July 23, 19___

Mr. Harvey Walker
Chemical Industries
Belletown, N.J. 00000

    Re: Smith Brothers Contract

Dear Harvey:

I wonder if there has been a slip-up in the mail service. I wrote you a query two weeks ago concerning the Smith Brothers contract we are considering, and we have not heard from you. I am becoming really concerned, because it is getting close to the time when we must make a definite decision on this. In the event you did not receive my detailed letter, I am enclosing a copy of it. As soon as you have read and digested this, please give me a ring at the Harrisburg office. I will be there until August 5th. On the 6th I leave for Toronto.

                          Cordially,

                          John Doe
                          Production Planning

Enc.

#54   (Letterhead)

September 4, 19___

Mr. James Anderson
Anderson Corp.
1719 Industrial Park Rd.
Bigtown, Tex. 00000

Dear Mr. Anderson:

August 1st I wrote you extending an invitation to attend a testimonial dinner to be given at the Northgate Hotel here for our Mr. Boise

Farnsworth on October 14th. I was almost sure you would wish to attend, but not having heard from you, I imagine that the invitation did not reach you. Since all reservations must be confirmed within a few days, I should appreciate it if you would wire or telephone me upon receipt of this letter. The dinner will be at 8:00 p.m. in the Gold Room, and will be formal, of course.

With very best regards,

Henry Roe
Invitations Chairman

Asking Forgiveness: Apologies

Apologies should be straightforward and sincere if they are to soothe ruffled feelings. Review your letter carefully to make sure you are not unconsciously implying that the customer is somehow at fault. It is usually better to write nothing at all than to take this destructive approach.

Below are several good letters of apology. The first is a follow-up of a case in which the customer had been sent merchandise she had not ordered. Worse yet, when she returned the merchandise it was sent back to her with a printed notice that no returned merchandise could be accepted without prior permission from the Adjustment Manager!

#55   (Letterhead)

February 2, 19____

Mrs. Beverly Morton
Fashion Store
Elegant Avenue
Middleburg, S.C. 00000

Invoice No.: 23794162

Dear Mrs. Morton:

I don't blame you for being angry about our double blunder in returning the unordered merchandise to you. Please allow me to apologize. I am not excusing our errors, but if you should ever again have to return merchandise from us that you have not ordered (and I sincerely hope you will not), please attach it to a letter or note addressed to me or your sales representative. This will assure acceptance and proper handling.

Regarding the current mess, please have the lot returned to us once more, marked for my attention. You will be promptly credited for the merchandise and the excess shipping charges.

Again, please let me say that I am very sorry for the inconvenience caused you. We do value your patronage and your friendship.

Sincerely,

John Doe
ADJUSTMENTS

The next letter concerns an itemized bill from an advertising agency which had been misunderstood by the customer. The one following it is self-explanatory.

#56   (Letterhead)

March 27, 19___

Mr. John Doe
New Food Packagers
1746 Camino De Le Reina
Valley Town, Calif. 00000

Re: Invoice 293184763

Dear Mr. Doe:

I want to apologize. It took me quite a while to figure out why you were so angry about our bill for the tentative labels, and then I realized it was a confusion regarding trade terms. "Production" in our business means something quite different from what it means in most other businessess. Our "Production Dept." takes care of assembling all the elements of an ad or a piece of artwork, doing pasteup and cleanup, and "producing" the finished job, ready for delivery.

We should have realized that "production" means something very different to someone not in our field, and used a more descriptive term. Of course this work requires considerable skill and experience, and does have to be billed. I hope you will agree with us now that this charge was reasonable.

I hope, too, that the finished label designs meet with your approval, and will help you achieve success in your new venture.

                                    Yours very truly,

                                    Richard Roe
                                    ACCOUNT EXECUTIVE

#57   (Letterhead)

                                    June 2, 19___

Mr. Henry Sutherland
2714 Greenleaf Lane
Suburbanville, La. 00000

Dear Mr. Sutherland,

A corrected statement of your account is enclosed. We are very sorry about the error in the previous one and hope that it did not cause you too much inconvenience. We double-check at every step in our processing of accounts, but somehow these things will happen on occasion. Please forgive us. We do appreciate your giving us the opportunity to serve you.

                                    Sincerely,

                                    George Doe
                                    CUSTOMER RELATIONS

Enc.

Sometimes a person is caught with no excuse for a misde-meanor. One may as well say so, when such is the fact, rather than trying to cook up some preposterous explanation. Utter frankness has a disarming and appealing quality.

#58   (Letterhead)

April 11, 19___

Prof. Reade Pendleton
c/o Prof. Henry James
2042 Academy Rd.
Smithville, Ohio 00000

Dear Prof. Pendleton:

I am embarrassed. There is absolutely no excuse for my not meeting you for our luncheon appointment today, or arranging to get word to you. I had the appointment written on my calendar, and I was looking forward to the occasion, but somehow I got it into my head that the date was for next Thursday. This was one of those days of a dozen crises that kept me away from headquarters.

Please forgive me this once. I am most anxious to talk with you. I will telephone you early next week in the hope that we can arrange another meeting before you leave—if you will trust me again.

Abjectly,

(Signed)   Richard Roe

The final apology letter is taken from an actual note sent by a very successful insurance agent to a couple he was trying to sell. He had gotten involved in one of those series of blunders that is almost comical, yet most serious to the hapless perpetrator. To the agent's surprise, the couple forgave him, although the insurance finally cost them $35 more than the last of two previous estimates he had given them.

This particular salesman's style is very informal and folksy at all times. His note of apology was handwritten on two sheets from a memo pad.

#59

6/24/___

Dot and George

Hi Folks,

Well after this you may not want to have anything to do with me any more—I made a final error on your homeowners' policy. The policy will cost you $265 a year for $75,000 insurance, $100 deductible—the same as the policy you now have, but it does give you more coverage.

I hate to make excuses, but we just added Tennessee to our agency and that's why I have had the problem. We write for five companies and each one is different.

I am very sorry. If you choose not to deal with me now I will certainly understand.

Kindest regards,

(Signed)   Walt

Not Asking, but Telling

Occasionally one is caught in a situation where he cannot ask for more time, but simply has to take it. Some material you are awaiting is late by a day or two days and you think you can rush and stay on schedule regardless. Then time stretches out and you find you are trapped and must be late. In such a case, write your customer, by all means, and let him know the situation.

Most printers that I have worked with, and many other outside companies on which one's business may have to depend think nothing of agreeing to a deadline date for delivery, then calmly letting the date pass. They rely on stalling the customer, and on fibs and flimsy excuses to cope with the situation. By doing this they often throw the unwary customer into an emergency situation, and irreparably damage their own relationship with the customer. It is much better to warn the customer of the impending delay, so that he can prepare to adjust. Here are two good letters that cover such contingencies.

#60 (Letterhead)

January 11, 19____

Mrs. Henry Richardson, Promotion Mgr.
Bonton Apparel Stores
1420 Broadway
New York, N.Y. 00000

Dear Mrs. Richardson:

The special vellum which you ordered for the invitations to your grand opening in Boston was delivered to us several days late. This, coupled with a temporary press breakdown, is going to make it impossible for us to deliver the invitations to you as promptly as we had hoped to. I am sorry, but we are going to be at least three days late. I hasten to let you know about this, so that you can make plans to cope with the situation in your own organization. If you wish, we can at least deliver the job a few boxes at a time, rather than waiting until the entire order is complete. Please let me know if you would like us to do this.

Again, let me say that I am sorry about this unavoidable delay.

Yours very truly,

Richard Roe
Cooperative Printers, Inc.

#61 (Letterhead)

March 23, 19____

Mr. Joseph Anderson, Supt.
Materials Dept.
Modern Methods Services, Inc.
Big City, Kansas 00000

Dear Mr. Anderson:

The trucking strike, which has been in the news these last several weeks, has played havoc with our production schedules. Some components of the D14JL Computers that we were supposed to install for you by April 20th have not been delivered to us even at this date, we regret to say. It is, thus, going to be impossible for us to deliver on time—in fact we cannot begin to estimate even an approximate date for delivery under present conditions. I want you to know that we are greatly distressed at the way things have gone, and we hope that no great dislocation is caused in your own business. I will certainly keep you posted on any developments.

Sincerely,

John Doe

In retail businesses, where unexpected delays are part of the routine, a brief form letter or postcard can be used for notification of the customers involved. That you do give the customer notice is the important thing. An example of such a form:

#62   (Store name and address)

Date

Dear Customer:

We are sorry, but we will be unable to deliver the merchandise you ordered (or left for repair) by the date promised, because of unavoidable delays. We now plan to deliver (date) _____. If this new date is not satisfactory, please telephone Miss Blair at 000-0000, Ext. _____ , so that a more convenient delivery date can be arranged.

Reason for delay: _____

(Signature)

Department Name

CHAPTER 5

Letters Regarding Assistance

Whether you are asking for assistance, offering it, or refusing it, your letter cannot be just a plain request or statement. It must have a certain amount of embellishment. Sometimes you must do a selling job. At other times great delicacy or diplomacy is required. Here are a variety of letters that should prove useful in many situations.

Asking for Assistance

#63 (Letterhead)

June 11, 19___

Mrs. Mary Stevens
3042 Water St.
Bigtown, Utah 00000

Dear Mary,

I have just about completed the financing for my company—corporation, rather. As a matter of fact we expect to have the stock oversubscribed within a couple of days. Now will begin the actual work of production, with all the complications that entails, but it will be happy work. Between Jim Brown's contacts and mine we have lined up plenty of competent help, and we expect to be well under way with the manufacturing in about three months. We also have the selling skills necessary.

I was going over our organization chart last night, rethinking the plans to make sure we had everything covered, and I did find one area in which we are a little weak. That area is advertising—and I now come to the point of this letter. Of course we shall put our account in the hands of an advertising agency, but I feel very uncertain about this important facet of the business. Neither Jim nor I has had the slightest brush with advertising. I know this is your field of expertise, and I am wondering if you could possibly find the time to give us a little guidance, at least in the beginning. We should expect to pay you a generous consulting fee on an hourly basis. What do you say?

Jim and I should like to discuss with you within a week or so the actual choice of an advertising agency, what we should expect from them, what sort of contract we should make, etc. Then, after the choice is made, we are hoping that you can go over the ads that are planned. We should like to have the benefit of your experience, your judgment, and your suggestions. I know of no one whose opinions I would consider more valuable.

Please let me know, Mary, if we can count on you for this aid.

> With warmest regards,
>
> (Signed)   Jack
>
> Jack Smith, President
> PIONEER FOOD CO., INC.

#64   (Letterhead)

> February 3, 19＿＿

Mr. William Johnson, Marketing Director
Excellent Products Co.
2412 Broad St.
Anytown, Ind. 00000

> Re: 100th Anniversary Plans

Dear Mr. Johnson:

Our 100th Anniversary, which is upcoming next January 14th, is such a milestone in the history of our company that Mr. Howarth and I feel we should have some sort of national celebration—something to really impress on the public the outstanding nature of our company. Perhaps there should be more than one angle. Certainly our employees should be included in the plans.

Due to the importance of this coming event, this letter is being sent to all department managers. We should like to have each of you give some thought to the celebration and submit a list of ideas. The deadline for such submissions will be <u>March 15th</u> of this year. I suggest that at least two weeks before that date you arrange a meeting with all of your people and ask them also to submit signed suggestions to you by March 8th or 10th. You can then send these on to me, together with your own signed suggestions.

The reason for the signing of these employee suggestions is that $5 will be paid for each general employee ideas that is sent in, whether or not it is used. Mr. Howarth, myself, and Mr. Jones of our advertising agency will then go over the ideas and select the ones we think should be put into effect for the celebration. Prizes will be awarded for the three that we think are outstanding. (If more than three are used we may award additional prizes.) As of now the prizes planned are:

First Prize—$100   Second Prize—$75   Third Prize—$50

Let's create some excitement about this great milestone in our company's history, let the country know about it. The best way to start is to get your own people fired up. I am counting on you. Remember, all entries must be postmarked March 15th or earlier.

Yours very truly,

Richard Roe, Vice Pres.

A letter similar to the above one might be written asking for suggestions on product names, on new ideas for product names, on time-saving new methods, or almost anything that is important to a viable business.

#65   (Letterhead)

September 11, 19___

Mr. Joseph Brown, Vice Pres.
Methods Supervision
Defense Products Co.
Los Arroyos, Calif. 00000

Dear Mr. Brown:

I read with great interest *The Wall Street Journal* article about the tremendous economies in time and labor you expect to achieve through the use of your new S41L computer. When I finished the article the thought occurred to me that you just might have a little idle time on that expensive machine—perhaps in the middle of the night or on weekends— and that you might be willing to make a deal whereby my company could tie in with the machine for an hour or so now and then.

As you know, we are a much smaller company, and do not compete with you in any way. However, even very brief access to such a computer would be of great value to us. Who knows, it might even speed some of the small components to you that are supplied by us!

Could we talk about this? If you think there is a possibility, I could meet with you at just about any time convenient to you. Probably a meeting at your office would be best. I shall look forward to hearing from you.

Yours very truly,

John Doe, Vice Pres.
COMPONENT MANUFACTURERS

In the preceding letter, it is not obvious that the component manufacturer is asking for help. He has disguised his plea as a business deal, which it is; but one that would be very beneficial to him, if the terms are right. The next letter is a simple request for help.

#66   (Letterhead)

March 10, 19____

Mr. Henry Anderson
Sales Dept.
Large Mfg. Co.
Industrial City, Mass. 00000

Dear Mr. Anderson:

I met you two years ago when I was with Jones & Co. in Boston and you sold us the typewriters for the main offices there. I have now changed companies, as you can see from the letterhead, and have relocated in nearby Belletown. I like it here, but current business conditions are making it rather difficult. Also, paper is a brand new field for me.

It just occurred to me the other night that you might be able to give me some assistance with leads, and perhaps with a few introductions. Since our products don't compete, but complement each other, we might work out a good system between us. (It will be of more value to you when I become established.)

Whether or not you can do this, I should certainly like to see you again. We used to have some good talks. How about letting me take you to lunch some time next week? Would Thursday be a good day for you? You name the place and the time. I will arrange to meet you wherever you say.

With very best regards,

George Smith
EXCELLENT PAPER CO.

Letters Offering Assistance

#67   (Letterhead)

March 11, 19____

Mr. George Smith
Sales Dept.
Excellent Paper Co.
5918 Engineers Rd.
Belletown, Mass. 00000

Dear George:

Your idea seems like an excellent one. Perhaps we can work something out. In any case, I shall be delighted to have lunch with you on Thursday of next week. Why don't you meet me at my office around noon and we'll take it from there. I'm anxious to hear all the gossip from my old stamping ground.

Sincerely,

(Signed)   Henry Anderson

#68   (Letterhead)

June 15, 19___

Mr. Jack Smith, President
Pioneer Food Co., Inc.
1217 Broad St.
Industrial Park, Utah 00000

Dear Jack,

I was delighted to hear that you have gotten so far along with the
organization of your new company. There is a real need for your products
and I am sure there are great days ahead for you and Jim. It will be a
pleasure to help you in any way that I can. Just let me know a week or so
ahead of time when you want to have a meeting.

With all best wishes,

Mary Stevens

#69   (Letterhead)

April 4, 19___

Mr. Raymond White
3742 Elegant Lane
Suburbantown, Ind. 00000

Dear Ray,

I was sorry to hear of the difficulties you have been having since leaving
Apex. The times aren't good, but with all your skills and your tremendous
background I am sure you will soon get connected.

If you think it will be helpful, I shall be glad to give you letters of
introduction to some influential people I know in your area. I am well
acquainted with Jack Hargreaves, for instance; and with Brent Mason of
the Big Cat Construction Machinery outfit. Several other names also come
to mind. Just say the word and I will shoot the letters off to you.

With very best regards,

(Signed)   John

#70   (Letterhead)

February 19, 19___

Mr. Richard Roe
Conscientious Bldg. Co.
912 Busy St.
Anytown, Ohio 00000

Dear Dick,

I think cement wall construction might be the answer to some of the cost problems you are running into on the Brookfield project. I have had considerable experience with pre-formed concrete and I should be glad to spend some time with you and discuss its possibilities, if you are interested. I could even help you out with the supervision in the beginning, or lend you one of our men, if the process appeals to you. I cannot forget how much help you gave to me years ago, when I was new in this area.

Sincerely,

(Signed)   Jerry

Asking for a Postponement in Giving Your Assistance

#71   (Letterhead)

February 19, 19___

Mr. Richard Roe
Conscientious Bldg. Co.
912 Busy St.
Anytown, Ohio 00000

Dear Dick,

You have caught me at just the wrong time with your request for help. We are working against a deadline and two of our men are laid up with injuries. I do want to help, however. I have an idea that cement wall construction might be the answer to some of the cost problems you are running into on the Brookfield project. This is not something you can just go into cold turkey, however; and I want to spend a lot of time with you discussing it before you make a move in that direction. You might even like me to help supervise in the beginning.

How much time have you? I won't be able to make a move in your direction for at least three weeks. Let me know if that will be okay and I will definitely put it on my calendar. It distresses me that I cannot get together with you immediately.

With warmest regards,

(Signed)   Jerry

Letters Refusing to Give Assistance

#72   (Personal Note, preferably handwritten)

March 14, 19___

Dear Joe,

I appreciate your predicament, and I would like to help, but you must know that my name would be mud if the news got around that I was giving out my clients' names for stock solicitation. Anyhow, I don't think that is the best way for you to go about your campaign, Joe.

Here is what I would suggest. What about good old Dun & Bradstreet? I think you are so bowed down with your series of difficulties that you are forgetting the common sense solutions. Buck up, fella. You are going to make it. Just go through your Dun & Bradstreet—at your bank, if you haven't got a copy—and you'll find all the dope on everyone in the state that might be a prospect for you.

Another idea is to get all the big town newspapers and take the names of the socialites, those who are running charity functions, etc., etc.

Suggestion #3: Why don't you take a few days off and relax, forget about everything. How about Belle and you coming up for the weekend of the 29th? I talked to Mary about it and she thinks it would be great. Let me know.

Best—

Hal

#73   (Letterhead)

March 25, 19___

Mr. John Doe, Vice Pres.
Component Manufacturers
Los Arroyos, Calif. 00000

Dear Mr. Doe:

I regret to say that we will be unable to let you make a tie-in with our
S41L Computer. It was especially designed for our operation, and just
about every minute is accounted for.

I would suggest, if you feel a vital need for this capability, that you
investigate some of the new telephone and satellite connections that are
available on a part time basis. If you are interested in these, I should be
glad to give you the information I obtained from some of them before we
decided on our own S41L.

Yours very truly,

Joseph Brown, Vice Pres.
Methods Supervision

#74   (Letterhead)

August 4, 19___

Mr. Walter Jones, Dept. Mgr.
Dept. 7
Complex Manufacturers
305 Suburban Rd.
Industrial Town, Md. 00000

Re: Changing Delivery Schedule

Dear Jones:

I regret to have to tell you that it will be impossible for this department to
make deliveries to you two days in advance of the present schedule. You
see, the deliveries we make to you depend on components we receive from
at least five different manufacturers. I cannot conceive of my being able to

persuade all of them to alter their schedules to accommodate this department. Sorry, old man. I hope the next time you ask a favor of me I will be able to grant it.

I do have one suggestion—not a very good one, I admit. If your whole new setup would depend on your receiving our deliveries on Mondays instead of Wednesdays, how would it work out if you just saved our material until the following Monday? Maybe that's a possibility.

With best regards,

John Smith
Manager, Dept. 6

#75   (Letterhead)

January 3, 19___

Mr. John Doe, President
Small Industrial Co.
1020 Main St.
Middletown, Ala. 00000

Dear Mr. Doe:

We regret to tell you that due to the present tight money situation we will be unable to grant the loan you requested. As I mentioned in our conversation the other day, this type of loan is not quite in our usual line, and the board has turned it down. We sincerely hope that you will be able to take care of your needs in some other way.

Yours very truly,

Richard Roe
Chief Loan Officer

Letters Trying to Dodge Giving Assistance, but Not Refusing

In the following letter John Smith, who wrote letter #74, decides instead not to refuse outright, but to try to dodge giving in to Walter Jones' request for a change in his schedule.

#76 (Letterhead)

August 4, 19___

Mr. Walter Jones, Dept. Mgr.
Dept. 7
Complex Manufacturers
305 Suburban Rd.
Industrial Town, Md. 00000

Re: Changing Delivery Schedule

Dear Jones:

I have given your request for a change in delivery schedule a great deal of thought, but it just does not seem to be practical from this end, as so many of our suppliers would be involved. The change would require trying to persuade all of the suppliers to revise their schedules—something close to impossible. It occurs to me also that reorganizing our department in this manner would probably absorb all the savings you achieve for Dept. 7.

I sympathize with your problem, of course, and I hope that there is another solution. If there is any other way we can help you, please let me know. Perhaps you could just hold over our Wednesday deliveries until the following Monday to fit them into your projected new setup. Whatever you decide, please keep me posted.

Cordially,

JOHN SMITH
Manager, Dept. 6

Other Examples of Qualified Refusals

#77   (Letterhead)

January 3, 19___

Mr. John Doe, President
Small Industrial Co.
1020 Main St.
Middletown, Ala. 00000

Dear Mr. Doe:

I have presented your loan request to the board, but without success. The members feel that today's tight money situation precludes granting the loan under exactly the conditions you outlined. If you wish to obtain an underwriter, or to furnish additional security, I am almost sure that we could work something out. Please let me know if you plan to proceed in either of those directions. We should very much like to be of service.

Yours very truly,

Richard Roe
Chief Loan Officer

#78   (Letterhead)

March 30, 19___

Mrs. Jean Evans
Elegant Shop
1512 Broad St.
Suburbanville, Pa. 00000

Dear Mrs. Evans:

I hasten to answer your letter concerning the antique toile reproductions, as I know that time is important to you and your customer. This type of upholstery fabric is completely out of our line, and I think that a specialist in this area could be much more helpful to you. By the time we found a source and placed a special order much time might be consumed, and the price might also be higher than through usual channels. If, in spite of this, you wish us to proceed, please send your instructions, together with pictures or samples, specific color description, etc. and we shall be happy to serve you.

Sincerely,

William Smith, Mgr.
Decorator Fabrics

Letters Suggesting Need for Assistance

Occasionally you must tell someone that he needs to get assistance, but you run a grave danger of irritating him if you do so. You must be firm and definite in your advice, yet use diplomacy. Here are several letters that make good use of the tactful phrase.

#79 (Letterhead)

September 8, 19___

Mr. James Johnson
1328 Business St.
Anytown, Ga. 00000

Dear Jim:

I am flattered that you should think I could advise you on a method of choosing stocks, but being a truthful guy, I must tell you that I have no formula. The successes I spoke of were a matter of plain, unadulterated luck; and like anyone else, I have had my share of losses in other markets. As a matter of fact, I doubt if I shall continue my amateur dabbling. It takes too much time, for one thing. I believe the standard advice, "Get a good broker" is probably the best there is—and of course that is no guarantee of profits.

Changing the subject, I was glad to hear that your business is doing so well. Things have just been fair here.

With very best regards,

(Signed)   Joe

#80   (Letterhead)

July 19, 19___

Mr. Robert Brown
3112 Home St.
Suburbanville, Mont. 00000

Dear Rob,

I was interested to hear of your plans for going into business for yourself, but I urge you to talk to a number of people in the field before you take the plunge. I have the greatest respect for your abilities, but _____ business is much more complicated than you might imagine, from what I have heard. You might avoid a great many headaches through a preliminary survey. If you plan to be in Chicago any time in the near future, I'd like to have you go over your plans with my friend Richard Roe. He will be able to give you a fairly complete picture, and will be glad to do so.

Let me know a little ahead of time when you are going to be here, and I will make an appointment for the three of us to have lunch together. You can take it from there.

With warmest regards,

(Signed)   Bill

#81 (Letterhead)

February 4, 19___

Mr. George Green
2418 Busy St.
Bigtown, Colo. 00000

Dear Green:

I regret to have to tell you that the extended time you say will be required on the Garrison job is absolutely out of the question. I suggest that you get some help on the project—subcontract part of it, under your personal supervision. If you would like to consider this and resubmit your estimate, I would be pleased. As you know, I am impressed with the quality of your work.

Let me know in the next day or so what you decide, but we must keep to the projected schedule.

Cordially,

Jack Wells
PRODUCTION MGR.

Recommending Someone Else to Give Assistance

#82 (Letterhead)

August 7, 19___

Mr. J.R. Brown
Apparel Mfrs.
7014 Seventh Ave.
New York, N.Y. 00000

Dear Mr. Brown:

I should very much like to help you, but fashions are absolutely out of our line. We specialize in hardgoods and furniture. I would suggest that you have your secretary telephone around and locate an agency that does specialize in fashions.

Yours very truly,

Harry M. White
SUPERIOR ART AGENCY

#83   (Letterhead)
                                                        September 22, 19___

Mr. Richard Roe, Jr., Gen. Mgr.
Richard Roe Stores, Inc.
949 Downtown St.
Detroit, Mich. 00000

Dear Sir:

You ask me whether you should introduce revolving charge accounts into the Richard Roe organization. Frankly, I do not feel qualified to give you a yes or no opinion on such a major factor in any retail business. I will say this, however, that these accounts, with their "high" interest rates, which were thought for many years to be a bonanza for retail businesses, are not now considered to be an all-around blessing. Modern, more scientific accounting practices have shown that in some businesses the revolving accounts do not pay their way.

For a valid opinion on the pros or cons concerning the value of introducing revolving charge accounts into your particular operation, I suggest that you get an expert econometric study made. There is an outfit right in your city which has a good reputation among retailers, although I have had no personal experience with them. Why don't you contact them and see what you think of their approach? The name is Credit Research Associates, and I believe they are on Water Street.

I hope that this suggestion will prove helpful to you in making your decision.

Yours very truly,

Pennington Brown, Comptroller
EMINENT STORES, INC.

CHAPTER 6

Letters Suggesting Change

Most people are extremely resistant to change. The mere suggestion that it may be necessary usually puts them on the defensive. Knowing this, you should tread softly and make a good case for whatever change you wish to accomplish. Study the approaches in the following letters.

Suggesting Change of a Person's Methods or Approach

#84   (Letterhead)

May 12, 19___

Mr. Henry Jones
4219 Olden Road
Anytown, Tenn. 00000

     Re: Sales technique

Dear Mr. Jones:

Your sales record for the first three months with our company has been exceptionally good, and I do not want to discourage you; however, I do want to give you a word of caution. A study of your accounts and a survey of your methods by Mr. Abbot suggests that you may be using too many high-pressure tactics. I should like to suggest that you tone down your approach a little, lean more to soft sell, even if this results in fewer sales in the beginning.

As you know, ours is an oldline, quality company, and we feel that the razzle-dazzle high-pressure approach can do harm to our image in the long run. As was demonstrated during our training sessions in Newark, we would rather you approach the customer as a friendly advisor rather than a salesman per se, studying his needs and tailoring your sales to them as exactly as possible. It is because of this policy that we do give a rather high beginning salary.

Think about it. Perhaps you are just over-eager; but with your intelligence and your basic selling skill I believe that you can adapt yourself to our methods and policy. You will find this an advantage in the long run, as it will cut down on returns and exchanges, and will create more long-term customers.

If you have any questions, please write me. Also, if you would like to have a few training sessions observing Mr. Abbot in action, this can be arranged. In any case, slow down a little. You are good. You don't have to press so hard.

> Yours very truly,
>
> John Doe
> Promotion Manager

#85   (Letterhead or
                                Store Memo Form)

July 10, 19___

A Letter to Our Sales Personnel
From the Training Director

Dear Co-Worker:

With competition becoming so keen, especially in these slow months, sales are hard to make. This is a fact that we all recognize, but we cannot just sit back and accept this. We must make that little extra effort, show that little extra skill that will increase sales figures, and incidentally increase your commissions.

I have a suggestion that I think you will find will turn quite a few "just lookers" into buying customers. I would like you to try this during the remaining days of July, and try to make a habit of it for use always. It is a simple thing, but it does take a little extra skill, a little extra effort. It has to do with the first words you speak to the potential customer.

What do you say now to a lady looking over a rack of dresses? Do you say, "Can I help you?" Many salespeople do, yet it doesn't do much to lead to a sale. It is too easy for the customer to make that deadly reply, "No, thank you; I'm just looking," sending you on your way.

For all the rest of this July I want you to forget that phrase. NEVER USE IT AGAIN. Instead, I want you to tell the customer something about the merchandise that she is examining, so that you create extra interest. If you are a good salesperson (and most of you are) this should not be difficult, because you have studied the merchandise in your department and you know all the interesting things about it.

Below are some sample phrases. Try them out, where they are appropriate, and make up some of your own to fit your department's merchandise. Enthusiastic, friendly remarks like these will increase the customer's interest in the merchandise. You can follow them up by asking what color she likes best, what size she is looking for . . . something that leads on toward a sale. Ask that follow-up question imediately, as shown here:

> Aren't these beautiful? They just came in this morning. What size are you looking for?

> These feel like silk, don't they, but they are made of Quiana, and they are wash-and-wear! Do you prefer the bright colors or the pastels?

> Aren't these prints marvelous? They look like handmade batiks. This one would look great on you. Would you like to try it on?

> Did you notice the beautiful workmanship on these? They were made to sell for a great deal more. What size do you wear?

There! I am sure you get the idea. Now make up some phrases of your own, and start using them. You will be amazed at their power in creating new sales for you.

Yours for success,

(Signed)   Jane Doe
Training Director

Suggesting Change of a Person's Appearance

#86   (Letterhead)

June 27, 19____

Mr. Richard Roe
3460 Suburban St.
Anytown, Mont. 00000

Dear Mr. Roe:

You passed the intelligence tests with flying colors and you scored well on the personal interview, except for one thing. As you know, Smith & Jones is a very conservative company, and it is a rule that men in the front office must be conservatively dressed. I am leaving the matter up to you. If you would care to give up your colorful dress and have your hair neatly styled—three-inch length—I think there would be a job here for you. What do you say? Please let me know immediately whether or not the change is agreeable to you, so that we can make a decision.

Yours very truly,

J.W. Smith, Jr.
Personnel Director

Suggesting a Change of Your Organization's Approach

#87   (Letterhead or Memo Form)

September 12, 19___

Mr. George Brown, Vice Pres.
Walter Jones & Co.
20719 Prestige St.
Bigtown, Ill. 00000

    Re: Conference on New Business

Dear Mr. Brown:

Since your very interesting interdepartmental meeting last week I have given a great deal of thought to your request for suggestions. During the meeting it seemed to me that most of the thoughts that were expressed concerned small things. Many of them would help in some degree, I am sure. However, I believe that the problem might be more basic, and I wonder what your opinion would be.

The whole approach of Walter Jones & Co. was formulated four decades ago, and it has worked very well up until now. However, I think that one of our troubles in recent years has been that we have not made an effort to attract the younger customer. By a simple matter of attrition, many of our old customers are dying off or retiring, and we are not attracting enough replacements.

I don't know exactly what the answer is to the problem, but I have been mulling over several ideas. I will just give them to you off the top of my head, and you can apply your seasoned judgment to them. Perhaps some of them will be worthy of roundtable discussion. Here goes:

1. What do you think of devoting some of our advertising to a theme something like this: "In your twenties? You Must Start Early If You Plan to Accumulate Wealth"?

2. I think perhaps our offices should be redecorated in more cheerful colors. Maybe even more modern furnishings.

3. The entrance to our offices is rather forbidding to someone not used to coming here. The answer might be to have a glass door, instead of the walnut, looking into more cheerfully decorated offices. Also, we might put something more than just our name on the door.

4. Maybe the agency could dream up a mailing piece directed to prosperous young homeowners or some professional list.

I hope that these ideas, or some variation on them, will be helpful, sir. I should be interested in your comments.

Respectfully,

William Brown

The cautious, deferential tone of William Brown's letter is a good one to take when you are asked to make suggestions. The danger in writing such a letter, even though suggestions have been requested, is that you may sound critical, conceited, or pedantic. Again, there is the not infrequent situation in which the man who asks for the suggestions does not really want them. The letter which pleases him most may simply say, in effect, "I don't really think it is anything we are doing which has caused the present condition. Every business in our field is having difficulties, and we are doing better than most." Consider carefully!

Suggesting a Change of Business Location

#88   (Letterhead or Memo Form)

September 12, 19___

Mr. George Green, Vice Pres.
Walter Jones & Co.
20719 Prestige St.
Bigtown, Ill. 00000

Dear Mr. Green:

Since our meeting last week when we discussed the matter of declining figures, I have been trying to come up with some ideas that might be helpful. The thought that finally came to me may be startling, but I think it is something we ought to talk about. Perhaps we should even have a study made.

Have you noticed, sir, the declining foot traffic in our area? It may just be that there is just too little going on in our section of the city nowadays, and we are losing off-the-street business. In other words, it may not be that our methods are faulty, but merely that our location has deteriorated. With so many businesses moving uptown in the last several years there are not enough feeder businesses left in this area. I know how you love the traditions of the old place, and I almost hesitate to make the suggestion, but perhaps Walter Jones & Co. should begin to consider a new location . . . or perhaps a branch office. May we talk about it?

Respectfully,

Joseph Anderson

The following one is a bolder, more determined letter from one friend to another.

#89 (Letterhead)

June 10, 19___

Mr. Henry Smith
The Gift Boutique
1046 Dull St.
Suburbanville, Ga. 00000

Dear Henry:

I was impressed with the beauty of your shop and the variety of interesting merchandise, but I think you are making a mistake to hang on in that location. Old rules of thumb like "it takes two years to get a business under way" can lead to disaster if you cling to them too slavishly. You yourself said the location is not too good, so why not leave it, and leave it now? Take some time out and find a really good spot?

I think the chain stores prove that that "two years" stuff is the bunk. I understand that if one of their new stores doesn't make it in six months, they move to another location. Of course they have the benefit of traffic and marketing studies, but you could do some of this yourself.

I hope you don't think I am being too forward in urging you to move, Hank, but you know, I am sure, that I have your best interest at heart. You have so much ability that I hate to see you trying to operate under less than optimum conditions.

With warmest regards,

(Signed)   Bill

Suggesting a Change of Methods or Systems

#90   (Letterhead)

February 15, 19___

Mr. Charles Clark, Gen. Mg.
Apparel Emporium
20742 Grand St.
Anytown, N.J. 00000

Dear Mr. Clark:

In line with our policy of trying to be helpful to the client, as well as performing a good audit, I have a suggestion to make which I think would be of benefit to your organization in these times. I should like very much to discuss it with you before you get very far into the new fiscal year.

In going over your accounts we were rather surprised to note that you are still using the LIFO system of inventory accounting. You doubtless adopted this long ago, during a period of rising prices. We feel, however, that in a period of declining prices you might find that the conservative FIFO system would offer certain advantages. I should be happy to point out the good features of the FIFO method if you are interested.

Thank you again for allowing us to serve you. I am looking forward to a long and happy relationship between our two companies.

Yours very truly,

John Diligent
Alert Auditors

#91 (Letterhead)

April 3, 19___

Mr. Joseph Wilson, Comptroller
Widespread Industry
9732 Industrial Rd.
Bigtown, Del. 00000

Re: Salesmen's expenses

Dear Wilson:

A man came into my office today selling a service that sounds very good to me. You might want to look into it—if you haven't already done so, this being more your field than mine.

The salesman was representing something called Instant Cash Letter. It presents a way of furnishing salesmen with ready cash or expense money on the road, without the need of having disbursement centers of our own, and without the use of checks. He claims that the average check issued by a company costs the company at least $2.50! And of course, as you know, money that is tied up at disbursement centers cannot be used for operating capital.

With the Instant Cash Letter the salesman can obtain money at any bank to pay expenses immediately—up to a certain limit. The I.C.L. people don't audit expense accounts, but merely bill the company for the total amount advanced. The salesman's own company audits expense accounts in the usual way. The big point is that all the usual checks to salesmen become unnecessary, and salesmen are never stranded waiting for money. The cost of the Instant Cash Letter service is said to be a mere fraction of the cost of those checks, and far less than the cost of funds tied up at distributing centers. It sounds great to me, and I thought I would pass on the information. I know you are always interested in anything that cuts the budget.

I am enclosing some literature the Instant Cash salesman left with me, and also his business card. If you write the company to have a representative call on you, you might mention this man's name so he will get credit.

I am looking forward to seeing you at next month's meeting. I hope your boy has fully recovered now from the effects of the accident. That was a terrible thing.

                                        Cordially,

                                        Richard Roe
                                        New England Branch Mgr.

Encs.

In the above letter note the deferential phrases and the warm, personal closing. It is probable that Richard Roe is going to bring up the matter of the Instant Cash Letters at the next interdepartmental meeting, but he is giving the comptroller a chance to get on top of the situation before he does so. He demonstrates that he has no wish to step on the comptroller's toes, yet is interested in all phases of the business.

Some Letters Suggesting Other Changes

The first letter below is a letter from an alert minor employee to an important executive. He seeks to help his company, and also to call attention to himself.

#92

                                        2770 Sawmill Rd.
                                        Littleville, Pa.
                                        March 3, 19___

Mr. Jon Jones, Promotion Mgr.
Adhesive Products
2900 Outer Rd.
Bigtown, Pa. 00000

Dear Mr. Jones:

I put a note about this in the suggestion box in our plant, but I feel so strongly about it that I thought I would write you a personal letter.
It seems to me, sir, that sometimes businesses get started doing something a certain way, and after that they just continue without ever taking a

second look. In this connection I am talking about some of our packaging. I went into a hardware store the other day looking for some of our wood adhesive for a little repair job I was doing at home. Believe it or not, I had a hard time locating our product among all the competing stuff they had there. I had never thought about it before, but our bottle looks just like everyone else's—in fact they all look alike! It struck me that this is a great mistake on everybody's part. A customer coming in to buy one product would be just as likely to pick up a competing product, either through natural laziness, or because it appears that there is no difference between the two.

I am sure there was some reason in the beginning to have the bottles look alike, but now that we are doing such a volume of business in the wood adhesive, I think we could really gain by making our package outstanding. You would be better able to judge just what changes should be made, but I had in mind something like a checkered bottle for our product, or a striped one, or even an entirely different shape. What do you think, sir?

Respectfully,

Henry Smith
Solid Products Div.

#93 (Letterhead)

June 12, 19____

Mr. John Doe, President
Adhesive Products
1432 Broadway
Metropolis, N.Y. 00000

Dear Sir:

I have been giving a great deal of thought lately to possible small moves that we could make to improve our business in this highly competitive period. It seems to me that this is an appropriate time to study our package design, for one thing. I have used our wood adhesive as an example.

As you know, when we introduced this product we were bucking up against Gordon's, which had the market to itself. Accordingly we designed our bottle to look as much like the established product as we legally could, for product recognition. The situation has now changed and the market is being divided among a half-dozen products, all of which are similarly packaged. I believe it is now time to do something to make the appearance of our bottle outstanding, so that the customer's eye will be attracted to it immediately when our bottle is placed among all the usual ones. (Oddly enough, just at the time I was considering this I received a suggestion letter from one of our help, Henry Smith, in the Solid Products Division, which was along the same lines.)

To illustrate the sort of design change I have in mind, I have had some sketches made that dramatize the possibilities in a distinctive, colorful appearance for the wood adhesive bottle. These are enclosed. I think such a change might add substantially to our business in this area, don't you?

As a matter of fact, I consider the experiment so successful that I should like to have your permission to do a survey of all our packaging design, with a view toward several profitable changes. I should appreciate it, sir, if you would have your secretary set up an appointment for me, so that you and we can discuss the question in detail. I shall look forward to hearing from you.

Yours very truly,

Jon Jones, Promotion Mgr.

Encs.

#94   (Memo Form or Letterhead)

January 15, 19___

Mr. Robert Watkins, Mgr.
Hobby Supply Center
1780 Craft Street
Anytown, N.M. 00000

Suggested Change of Store Hours

Dear Watkins:

The suggested change of store hours which was discussed at our quarterly meeting has now been thoroughly tested in our main store and we find it has many advantages. The mere fact that traffic is lighter at 10:00 a.m. has cut down on reports of employee accidents. The later opening hour has also reduced tardiness and eliminated any excuse for a morning coffee break. The resultant saving in time has actually increased sales slightly, while making a significant reduction in occupancy costs. Employees are also happy with the change. There have been few objections to the later

Friday closing, since overall the employees have gained two hours of additional free time. (Women employees are particularly grateful for this.) All things considered, we think that changing the store hours is a wise move, and Mr. White and I now request that all stores make this experiment for two months, reporting on results at the next quarterly meeting. Please make the necessary changes in the enclosed advertising notices, inserting your store name and address, and arrange with the local newspapers to run the ads as soon as possible. We also suggest that you notify all your employees of the projected change immediately. Of course you will also have to notify the newspapers and all suppliers of the change in hours. Your full cooperation will be appreciated.

New Hours Schedule

Monday through Thursday—10:00 a.m. to 5:30 p.m.

Friday—10:00 a.m. to 9:00 p.m.

Saturday—10:00 a.m. to 5:30 p.m.

As part of the experiment it is important that you keep account of comparative sales figures day by day and note any other important results. If you have any comments or any questions concerning the program, please let me hear from you.

Yours very truly,

Richard Roe
Operations Manager

Encs.

CHAPTER 7

Letters Concerning Advice

"If you'll take my advice, you'll forget it" . . . hackneyed words, these, from many a movie and TV script. And if you'll take *my* advice, you'll forget them! Unless the giving of advice is mere ego-balm for the giver, it must be skillfully and diplomatically done. This is especially important when advice is volunteered.

First of all, the advisor, unless he is very careful, may seem to put himself in an exalted position. He makes a claim that his judgment is superior to that of the advisee. For another thing, he is often interfering with something the other person wants to do very much. A negative reaction is almost guaranteed. This is particularly true in the case of young people.

One good way of avoiding both these unfortunate positions when you give advice is to credit the advice to someone else. If this is impractical, be sure you are tactful and deferential.

120

Some Model Letters Giving Advice

#95   (Letterhead)

                                                      May 3, 19___

Mr. John Doe
3456 Prosperous St.
Suburbantown, La. 00000

Dear John:

I was impressed with the detailed nature of the organization plans for your new business. I can't see anything you have over-looked, but of course that is not my field.

I do have one thought which you might want to consider. I noticed the salaries you projected for various technicians and junior executives were at the bottom of the scale. I assume you plan to take on inexperienced people and train them. I wish you would think twice about this. I have known several companies that went this route, and they found it entailed innumerable headaches.

You may save on actual salaries, but you have to consider the length of time that such help will be non-productive—sometimes even obstructive. There is also the cost of your time and that of other executives which is taken up in training these people. In the end you may find you have spent more in this way than you would have spent on salaries for thoroughly experienced help. In some cases many of the trainees may even turn out to be duds.

There is another angle to consider here, too, and that is that when you start your business you want to get under way as soon as possible and begin producing. Please think about all this. I feel that you will have enough to do in the beginning without taking on additional problems.

I must say I admire your courage and initiative. Whether you take my advice or not, I am sure you will come out on top. You have a great idea. Keep me posted. I want to be on hand for the opening celebration.

                                        With warmest regards,

                        (Signed)   Charles

#96   (Letterhead)

April 7, 19——

Mr. Richard Small
Small Mfg. Co.,
920 Outlying St.
Anytown, Ind. 00000

Dear Richie:

I was happy to hear that your business is coming along so well, but I was rather surprised to note that you are considering buying fork lifts and other heavy equipment. Out here nearly everybody rents such equipment as needed. By doing this you avoid a substantial capital investment and you don't have to provide for upkeep—if a machine breaks down, you just call the equipment company and they send out a replacement. We find it saves a lot of trouble and delay.

Of course I don't presume to be telling you your business. You have certainly managed very well so far. I just wanted to suggest that you look into the rental thing, if you haven't already done so.

When are you going to be in Wichita? Perhaps you could bring Mary with you and the four of us could paint the town. It would be like old times. Rose would like that.

With very best regards,

(Signed)   Joe

#97   (Letterhead)

September 3, 19——

Mr. Richard Roe
Roe Industries
27 Industrial Park
Negocio, Calif. 00000

Dear Mr. Roe:

I am flattered that you should ask my opinion on the proposed solutions to your company's financial dilemma. I am certainly not a financial expert, although I have been through a similar situation, with John Doe Corp., as you know. I will tell you some of the things we did, and perhaps that will be helpful to you in making your own plans.

Frankly, it seems to me, with the relatively small amount of money you need, that trying to sell more stock at this time is not the answer. If you are actually ready to go into production with the new quick-dry cement, which you feel will bail you out of your difficulties, I suggest you concentrate on that one objective—with as little "sharing of the wealth" as possible.

There are two things we did at John Doe, and from what you have shown me I see no reason why you cannot do the same. (Of course you have to use your own very good judgment.) The two-step process is relatively simple, yet when one gets into a financial bind, it's the sort of thing that sometimes doesn't come to mind. Here is what we did, and I feel sure you can do it:

(1) We told our creditors the situation and asked them to agree to defer payments three to six months. We had no difficulty here. They all agreed.

(2) We offered a 10% discount in an end-of-the-year sale for prepayment: Our regular customers leaped at this, and we raised $150,000.

If you could offer the same sort of discount on your best-selling products, you would have the cash in hand to produce the new cement. If this is pre-sold, there is your answer. In the event you do need even more money, however, you might consider offering convertible preferred stock, rather than the common. I understand that offers good possibilities and it does not dilute your holdings.

So there you have it. That's all the advice this old warhorse can give you. I hope it helps to solve your problem. Lord knows you deserve to be able to hold on to that new cement formula. Please let me know what you decide, and if there are any questions I can answer, don't hesitate to call on me.

Cordially,

Henry Jones

P.S.   I am returning your material under separate cover.

Enc.

Letters Accepting Advice

There is little difficulty here, except that these letters should always be gracious. Some egotists occasionally ask for advice, then when it is given they shoot back word that they have already thought of the same solutions! If it is true, and you feel you must say this, at least qualify it a little, as in the following letter.

#98   (Letterhead)

April 20, 19___

Mr. Joseph Anderson
Progressive Mfg. Co.
Bigtown, Kans. 00000

Dear Joe:

Thanks for your suggestion about renting the fork lifts instead of buying outright. The funny thing is that I had just about decided to do that when your letter arrived, but I couldn't quite make up my mind. Your point about repair troubles when a company owns its own machines was something I had not thought about. I have now definitely decided to go the rental route.

Give our regards to Rose. Mary and I miss you folks, but it will probably be months before I can get away for a trip. I'll let you know pronto if an opportunity turns up.

Best,

(Signed)   Richie

The next letter is a straightforward thank you, showing warm appreciation.

#99 (Letterhead)

September 9, 19___

Mr. Henry Jones
Parts Mfg. Co.
Los Angeles, Calif. 00000

Dear Mr. Jones,

I can't tell you how much I appreciate your suggestions on a program to relieve our financial bind. As soon as I read your letter I knew that you had given me the solution, and I immediately fired off letters to all our creditors, inviting them to a meeting. I am sure that I can get them to work with me when I demonstrate the potential of the new cement formula.

I expect to be in L.A. on the 17th and I should like to stop by and thank you personally. I will telephone you from the station, and perhaps we can have lunch together.

Gratefully,

Richard Roe

Letters Refusing Advice

These should also be thank-you letters, and they should be carefully written to avoid the impression that you are snubbing the advisor. Any thoughtfulness deserves appreciation—and, who knows, you may need help from this same advice source at some later date. Here are some well written refusals of proffered advice:

#100   (Letterhead)

August 7, 19___

Mr. James Mallory
Miscellaneous Manufacturing Co., Inc.
3040 Industrial Rd.
Busytown, Md. 00000

Dear Mr. Mallory,

Thank you for your suggestions regarding the problem at the Gainesville plant. I shall certainly give them careful consideration. Things are beginning to look better at Gainesville, however, and I may end up making no changes at this time. In any case, I want you to know that I do appreciate your concern. I will let you know what develops.

Sincerely,

George Smith

The phrase, "I'll let you know what develops" lends conviction to the rest of Smith's letter, but he may conveniently forget to follow through on it if he wishes.

#101   (Letterhead)

April 20, 19___

Mr. Joseph Anderson
Progressive Mfg. Co.
Bigtown, Kans. 00000

Dear Joe,

Thank you for your thoughtful letter regarding the advisability of renting fork lifts and other heavy equipment, but it came just a little too late. We had already contracted for several of the lifts and some are already at work. I can see that the rental idea is a good one, however, and I may regret not having gone that route.

Give our regards to Rose. Mary and I miss you folks, but it will probably be months before I can get away for a trip. I'll let you know pronto if an opportunity turns up. In the meantime, let's keep in touch.

Best,

(Signed)   Richie

Letters Expressing Appreciation for the Results of Advice Given

---

#102   (Letterhead)

May 23, 19___

Mr. George Atwood
John Doe Co.
Birmingham, Ala. 00000

Dear George:

I feel like I ought to give you a medal or a reward or something. I took your advice on the Farwell matter and it worked like a charm. I thought you would like to know. I will fill you in on the details when I see you in July. In the meantime, write me—and if there is any favor I can do you, don't hesitate to call on me.

With warmest regards,

(Signed)   Henry

#103   (Letterhead)

February 15, 19___

Mr. John Wise, Pres.
Big Industries
New York, N.Y. 00000

Dear Mr. Wise:

I got to thinking the other day that I owe you a tremendous vote of thanks.

I took your advice concerning diversification back in 1970 and the chemical plant we acquired at that time has given us an invaluable flexibility during the present difficult period. Who could have foretold that the Japanese were going to give us such stiff competition in the other areas? Or did you have a feeling about it?

You may not even remember our conversation about diversification at the Manufacturers Club dinner so long ago, but I was very much impressed with your advice. I went back and sold the Board, and we have had nothing but good results. Thank you again.

Yours very truly,

(Signed)   John Doe Industries

Warning Against a Source of Advice

Warnings against anything have to be carefully worded to avoid possible legal problems. However, what you cannot say outright can often be implied, as the following letter illustrates. If you have any doubt at all about the letter you wish to write, check with your legal department.

#104   (Letterhead)

May 12, 19___

Mr. Henry Smith
Competitive Products
Anytown, Wisc. 00000

Dear Smith:

I was rather astounded to hear that you are going ahead with plans for a new division on the basis of advice from one source. I strongly urge you to discuss the matter with others in the field. The man you mention is a tremendous promoter. I take it for granted that you have contacted all references and checked with Dun & Bradsteet.

With warmest regards,

John Doe, Vice Pres.

CHAPTER 8

Models for Letters of

Acceptance and Refusal

Making your meaning crystal clear, whether delicately or bluntly, as the situation requires, is important in letters of acceptance and refusal. Some require skillful wording to avoid legal entanglements. A special note is made of cases where this is likely to be so. In any situation that you suspect may have a legalistic angle you are advised to get expert counsel. It is much better to be counseled ahead of time than to make an error and then seek to be extricated from the resulting tangle.

An Enthusiastic Response to a Business Offer

#105 (Letterhead)

September 2, 19___

Mr. R. T. Smith
Marketing & Sales
Modern Components
2112 Broad St.
Industrial City, N.M. 00000

Dear Mr. Smith:

Your offer sounds very interesting. I suggest that we get together and thrash out details. After we have settled all points between us, the lawyers can draw up a final agreement. This will keep the record straight and protect both of us.

I can set aside either Wednesday or Thursday afternoon, October 21 or 22, for our conference. Please write or telephone me as soon as possible and let me know which date will be convenient for you. If it is agreeable to you, I think that holding the discussions in my office will be best, so that all files and figures will be available.

Yours very truly,

Richard Roe

The above letter, for all its casual, spontaneous tone, is very carefully written. The writer makes sure to say that all discussions so far, and those planned, are merely preliminaries leading up to a written agreement. This is one of the situations where the writer might inadvertently bind or obligate himself if he were not careful. He has doubtless checked his letter with the legal department.

Other Model Letters Accepting Business Offers

#106   (Letterhead)

May 4, 19___

Mr. George Smith
Marketing Div.
Appropriate Mfg. Co.
7942 Distant Rd.
Bigtown, Minn. 00000

Re: Parts for FL46107

Dear Mr. Smith:

If you can furnish the parts exactly as described in the specification sheet you left with me (or "exactly like sample"), in the quantity, and on the dates you mention in your letter of April 28, you have a deal. We will need:

4,000 of the A4719 Silicon Wafers on or before April 15, 19___.

And 4,000 more on or before June 1, 19___.

10,000 of the X247B Amplification Units on or before June 1, 19___.

All items furnished must conform to appropriate Milspecs, copies of which are attached hereto, and random samplings must pass our standardized tests as described in my letter of April 23. Please include these points in the sales contract you send to me for signing. I shall look forward to hearing from you soon.

Yours very truly,

John Doe, Mgr.
Parts Procurement Div.

Encs.

Once again, note that this letter is carefully written, so that it cannot be construed as an order or a contract in itself. Check such letters with your lawyer.

#107   (Letterhead)

August 3, 19___

Ms. Jane Doe
Jane Doe Interior Decorators
8942 Park Ave.
New York, N.Y. 00000

Dear Ms. Doe:

I have gone over your sketches and plans for The Westbury Arms with the management and we are pleased with them. However, we feel that your price is somewhat out of line. If you could manage to shave the price by about 15% without sacrificing the general appearance or the feeling of quality, I believe we could come to an agreement, and the work could be started immediately. Please telephone me as soon as you receive this letter and let me know the prospects for this. Of course, if there are changes in materials, we will have to have another conference. If we come to an agreement—and I am quite sure we shall—we can draw up a contract at that time.

Thank you for taking so much pains with our problem. You are a very talented lady, and I look forward to working with you in the near future.

Sincerely,

Richard Roe
Manager, Quality Hotels

Some Letters Accepting Suggestions

#108   (Letterhead)

June 18, 19___

Mr. Jon Jones, Promotion Mgr.
Adhesive Products
1219 Way St.
Newark, N.J. 00000

Re: Changing Package Designs

Dear Jones:

I am enthusiastic about your idea of changing package designs for our products. I think such a change may prove a real shot in the arm for some of our lines. In several cases the changes would be merely cosmetic; but there are others, I am sure, that could even have package improvement. Both types of change could give a fresh theme to our advertising.

As you probably know, the next Board Meeting is scheduled for September 1st. Do you suppose you could be ready with sketches and plans for changes in the design of four or five products at that time? Costs should be included. (The sketches you sent me could be part of the group.) You and I should get together and go over the presentation several days before the meeting. Let me have your answer concerning the feasibility of this within the next day or so.

I am glad you mentioned Henry Smith to me. I am sending him a commendation award.

Very truly yours,

John Doe, President

A more tentative response to the same suggestions might read as follows:

#109 (Letterhead)

June 18, 19____

Mr. Jon Jones, Promotion Mgr.
Adhesive Products
1219 Way St.
Newark, N.J. 00000

Dear Jones:

I think there may be some merit in your suggestion that we make changes in our package designs, but I should like to have more facts and figures. Can you cite me some costs? Also, some consumer studies might be in order to see whether the changes are justified. For a beginning, I suggest you run a small scale test on the new wood adhesive designs, and score them against our present package. Please call me as soon as you have the results.

Very truly yours,

John Doe, President

Presenting a Counter-Proposal
Without Turning Down a Suggestion

#110 (Letterhead or In-House Memo Form)

April 9, 19____

Mr. A.B. Cee, Parts Engineering
Aero Co.
7918 Industrial Road
Factoryville, Mo. 00000

Re: 16-234792-966 Wafer Pack

Dear Cee:

I can understand your concern about accepting the re-worked Wafer Packs. I am inclined to agree with your opinion, although taking this position would cost us greatly in delay. It occurs to me that there may be a compromise solution.

I suggest you have Triangle re-seal ten of the Wafer Packs in the manner they suggest and deliver them to Quality Control. Let Q.C. then have them assembled in simulated operational status, and have the finished product subjected to a 120-hour operational test. If the Wafer Packs pass this retesting, I believe it will be safe for us to accept the entire lot of reworked Wafer Packs — again subject to all routine tests.

If Triangle will not agree to this sample testing, we have no choice but to wait for the entire 200 to be replaced, and I believe you should stand firm on this.

Clark Roe, Vice Pres.

The above letter, as you may have noted is the answer to letter #51 in Chapter 4. It is polite, brief, and unequivocal. Vice President Roe takes entire responsibility concerning the matter of the questionable Wafer Packs. If he had wished to avoid taking entire responsibility, he could have said in the second paragraph, "If in *your opinion* the reworked Wafer Packs pass this retesting satisfactorily, I believe it will be safe for us to accept the entire lot . . ."

Letters Accepting a Change in Contract Specifications

Here again is a case in which you would be wise to have legal advice. Notice the clarity and specific nature of the following letter. The writer also asks for an answer, just to make sure there is no misunderstanding.

#111   (Letterhead)

March 3, 19___

Mr. Henry Jones
Good Builders, Inc.
3310 Broad St.
Bigtown, Kans. 00000

Dear Mr. Jones:

I have examined the Lees carpet samples you left with me and I have decided it will be quite all right to substitute #2912 in the Woodland

Green for the Quality Line carpeting specified in our contract for the new building on Grant St. Of course all other features of our contract still hold, including your 10-year guarantee on the carpeting. Am I correct in assuming that the carpet guarantee still holds?

Yours very truly,

Jane Doe

Letters Accepting an Offer of Help

#112   (Letterhead)

October 14, 19___

Mr. Robert Smith
2024 Suburban St.
Anytown, Ga. 00000

Dear Bob:

It was great of you to offer to pick up and deliver those machines to Atlanta for me. I don't know how I could have managed to make the trip myself with this broken arm, much less load and unload the things. You will probably save me the good will of the customer, too.

I will wait here for you Thursday night, and I will have my office boy stay also, so he can help load the machines in your station wagon. It will be best if you come to the side entrance on Lamont St. I will see you there around 7:00 p.m. Don't worry if you can't get there on the dot.

Thanks again, old friend. I hope you are telling the truth when you say you are not making a special trip to do this for me. And I hope I can do something to repay you in some measure one of these days.

Sincerely,

(Signed)   Harry

#113   (Letterhead)

June 17, 19___

Miss Jenny Jones
Records Dept.
Miscellaneous Corp.
1020 Broad St.
Anytown, Md. 00000

Dear Miss Jones:

I hate to put you to the trouble of sorting out and Xeroxing all the insurance records of Albert E. Johnson, but I will be most grateful if you will do this and send the copies on to me. It was generous of you to suggest this solution to the problem. As you may have guessed, I am working against a deadline, and without your help I would not be able to complete the study on time. Thank you very much.

Sincerely,

John Doe
Statistical Dept.

Letters Accepting a Recommendation of Someone

As a rule one does not wish to go all out and promise a solid job to someone who has been recommended. The following two acceptances give the prospective employer an out, in case the new employee proves to be unsuited to the job.

#114   (Letterhead)

March 3, 19___

Mr. Henry Devereux, Marketing Div. Mgr.
Miscellaneous Products Co.
2442 Blank Rd.
Bigtown, Or. 00000

Dear Henry:

I will be happy to interview Miss Jane Smith. If she can cope with our complicated terminology, she may have a job here. We are almost always on the lookout for good secretarial help and your recommendation is impressive.

Cordially,

Mark Hanson
CUSTOMER EDUCATION

#115   (Letterhead)

February 3, 19___

Mr. Richard Roe
Executive Service Co.
Port City, Ca. 00000

Dear Mr. Roe:

I was interested in your description of Mr. John Doe III's background. I will be glad to join the two of you for luncheon on the 8th, but of course you know we shall be considering other candidates during the same period. The man chosen must have high executive capacity and extremely varied experience. In addition to being in charge of the Washington office he will be responsible for legal, industrial and governmental relations. Please reflect on these facts and confirm our luncheon appointment with my secretary if you still believe Mr. Doe may be the person we need.

Yours very truly,

Robert Smith, President

Letters Refusing to Accept an Offer

#116   (Letterhead)

June 3, 19____

Mr. John Smith
Sales Dept.
Merchandise Co., Inc.
3047 Broad St.
Anytown, N.J. 00000

Dear John:

Thank you for giving me advance notice of the closeout of seconds, but we are not a prospect for this type of merchandise. We would not use it even in a special sale, as the customer it would attract would not be interested in our regular merchandise, and our reputation might be damaged. I do appreciate your thinking of me first, however.

Yours very truly,

MERCHANDISE MANAGER

#117   (Letterhead)

March 27, 19____

Mr. George Ryan
Good Printers, Inc.
9022 Vine St.
Bigtown, S.C. 00000

Dear Mr. Ryan:

The paper sample you sent me is not suitable for our job, even though you could furnish it at the same price as the cheaper one we requested. Its extra weight would increase the postage to such an extent that the total cost of the mailing piece would be considerably higher.

I am afraid we will have to count your company out on this particular job, because production time allowed is so short. In the meantime a bid has been submitted by another printer, and he has our stock available.

Thank you for your efforts, in any case. I will let you know when another job is in the offering. I always enjoy dealing with you.

Cordially,

Frank Smith
Advertising Mgr.

Letters Refusing to Accept an Offer of Help

In a situation in which you feel you must turn down an offer of help, and yet do not wish to explain why, there are a number of phrases that will serve. Any of them can be used in the following letters, as indicated.

#118 (Letterhead)

February 10, 19___

Mr. Richard Roe
Prosperous Outfit, Inc.
2027 Blank Rd.
Anytown, Ill. 00000

Dear Roe:

It was good of you to offer assistance and I deeply appreciate it; however, I feel that I must *work things out within the organization.* * I am mapping out plans now, and I will let you know what develops.
Again—thank you.

With warmest regards,

---

*For the italicized words in the above letter any phrases like the following may be substituted. (They should not, of course, be italicized or underlined in your letter.)

operate within my own resources.
work things out on this end.

give the problem more time to resolve itself—and it looks as if it may.

seek a long-term solution.

#119   (Letterhead)

January 3, 19___

Mr. John Doe
Bigtime Industries
7482 Easy St.
Anytown, N.Y. 00000

Dear John Doe:

Thank you so much for your offer of help, but the picture is not quite so bleak as I must have inadvertently painted it. Actually, two solutions have occurred to me since I talked to you. (It could be that you inspired them.) In any case, I certainly appreciate your generous concern. Perhaps you will allow me to take a raincheck, in case I do need you after all.

With deepest appreciation,

Richard Roe

A Refusal to Accept Responsibility for an Error

#120   (Letterhead)

October 15, 19___

Mr. Robert Jones, Gen. Mgr.
Miscellaneous Products Co.
1041 Anonymous St.
Anytown, Kansas 00000

Dear Mr. Jones:

I am sorry that production has been disrupted in Dept. M4, but we followed that department's instructions to the letter, as we read them. It never occurred to anyone along the line that the instructions could be interpreted two ways. I am enclosing a photocopy of the order to show what I mean.

It has never been required up until this time, but I think in the future I will always double-check important orders like this by telephoning the department head. Of course this does not help the present situation, but if you or Mr. Doe can think of any way I can assist in unraveling the snarl I shall be most happy to do so. Please let me know.

Respectfully,

Richard Roe

Enc.

#121   (Letterhead)

June 3, 19___

Mr. Robert Smith
Fancy Merchandise Co.
110 Busy St.
Anytown, N. C. 00000

Re: Error in Order No. 4497645

Dear Mr. Smith:

We are extremely sorry that you did not receive the merchandise you wanted for your Midsummer Fair promotion, but as you can see by the copy of your order which is enclosed, someone inadvertently wrote down the wrong stock number.

You will be happy to know that the correct merchandise was shipped by air freight within an hour of your telephone call to me. You should have it tomorrow. The other merchandise, if you cannot use it, should be returned to us for credit to your account.

Yours very truly,

Roy Brown, Mgr.
Customer Relations

Enc.

In both the above letters, although he firmly disclaims responsibility for the error, the writer avoids being accusatory and does his best to ameliorate the situation.

Refusing to Take Responsibility for a Course of Action

Refusing to take responsibility in advance can often be done quite subtly, so as not to create a confrontation. All you need do is say, "This is what I would do in such a case, *but use your own judgment.*" The latter phrase takes you off the hook.

The skillful use of a similar device is discussed earlier in this chapter, regarding the letter form Clark Roe to A. B. Cee. See # 110.

The following letters are on different angles.

#122   (Letterhead)

April 3, 19___

Mr. Leonard Green
Diversified Co.
742 Industrial Rd.
Anytown, N.J. 00000

Dear Mr. Green:

I am terribly sorry that things did not work out the way you and I had hoped they would, but I am surprised that you seem to blame me. You asked me for suggestions and I gave them in a friendly spirit; however, I clearly told you that you had to use your own judgment and that the decision was up to you. That is the only way it could be, as you certainly knew more about your business than I did. If you will look over my letter of last November 10, you will see that this is so.

Well, no matter. I certainly hope now that you can cut your losses and come out with enough for a new beginning. I know that you are going to make it big one of these days.

With best personal regards,

John Doe

The next letter is a definite, outright refusal to take responsibility for someone else's future action.

#123 (Letterhead)

October 11, 19___

Mr. J.A. Smith
Small Business, Inc.
Anytown, Mo. 00000

Dear Smith:

As you say, there are two ways that you can go, but I cannot take the responsibility of advising you. For one thing, I do not know enough about the inner workings of your company. I do have a suggestion, however, and that is that you call in a team of professional business consultants. Even then, of course, the final decision will be up to you.

Sorry, old fellow, that I can't be more helpful, but that is the way it is. I do want you to know, though, that you have my heartfelt best wishes. I'm pulling for you.

Cordially,

John Doe

Refusing to Take Responsibility in the Case of an Unwarranted Use of Product

---

#124 (Letterhead)

May 22, 19___

Mr. Robert Johnson
2032 Outer Rd.
Suburbia, Miss. 00000

Dear Mr. Johnson:

Comparison will show that Reputable Products has one of the best warranties in the field, giving the widest coverage, but we do not cover the use of our Precision Drill No. 419 in any manner not specified in the warranty. If we did so, the price of our drill would have to be increased astronomically.

Now about the difficulty with your drill. The chuck has been damaged. We can replace this for you at relatively low cost to you—$4.85, including postage—and return the drill to you within two weeks. If you wish us to do this, please check the proper box below, sign, and return this letter in the enclosed envelope. (If you do not wish to have this work done, please check the other box, and enclose 65¢ return postage.)

Sincerely,

Jane Doe
WARRANTY & REPAIRS DIV.

_____YES. Please make repairs   _____NO. Please return merchan-
and charge me as specified above.   dise to me without repairs.

_____   _____
Customer signature   Customer signature

Refusing to Honor Expired Warranty

#125   (Letterhead)

January 10, 19___

Mrs. Rita Roe
1011 Prosperous St.
Amity, N.M. 00000

Dear Mrs. Roe:

We regret to have to tell you that the warranty has expired on the Excellent Electric Scissors which you sent us for repair under warranty. This model (No. XL5) was discontinued three years ago, indicating that the two-year warranty would have definitely expired, even though you have no salescheck.

If you like, we can repair the scissors for you at a nominal charge, $2.50, and return them to you within thirty days. Repairs include new super-sharp blades, oiling and adjusting. The scissors will be like new

Please check the appropriate box on the instruction card enclosed, sign, and return the card to us immediately. We will follow your instructions.

Sincerely,

Kathie Harris
CUSTOMER RELATIONS

#126 (Letterhead)

April 29, 19___

Mrs. J.J. Gurney
7042 Park Place
Suburbia, Colo.00000

Dear Madam:

We are sorry, but the warranty has expired on your Derby Vacuum Cleaner, model 241Z. The warranty card which you mailed to us when the Vacuum Cleaner was purchased indicates that the purchase was made from Wright Bros. on February 21, 19___. It expired one year from that date, or two months ago.

For prompt and expert repair of your Derby Vacuum Cleaner at minimum cost, please take your Vacuum Cleaner to one of our authorized service centers in your area. A list of our service centers is enclosed.

Respectfully,

Service Representative

Enc.

#127 (Letterhead)

June 23, 19___

Mr. Robert Jones
3447 Pleasant Lane
Big City, Ka. 00000

Dear Mr. Jones:

We are sorry, but you seem to have misread the warranty on your Blanko Color TV Set, model XR33. If you will recheck the warranty you will note that both parts and labor are covered for two years, but the extended warranty for the next three years (featured only by Blanko) does not cover labor. It does promise payment for any parts that may be needed. A check to cover our portion of the bill is enclosed.

Sincerely,

Service Dept.

Enc.

Refusals Concerning Contracts

As you know, any letters concerning a contract should be checked with a lawyer, lest you inadvertently void the contract or involve yourself in other difficulties. These sample letters are for approach and phrasing only.

#128

1029 Opulent Ave.
Suburbantown, Kans. 00000
April 29, 19——

Mr. Richard Roe
Able Contractors
9012 Busy St.
Distant City, Kans. 00000

Dear Mr. Roe:

I am sorry that your expenses are running beyond expectations on the duplex you are building for me at 17 Sunshine Way, but I feel that this is your responsibility according to the contract. I have budgeted my funds according to the figures you gave me and am in no position to allot additional money to this project.

Sincerely,

Jane Doe

#129 (Letterhead)

May 10, 19___

Mrs. Jane Doe
1029 Opulent Ave.
Suburbantown, Kans. 00000

Dear Mrs. Doe:

If you will reread the contract for the duplex on your property at 17 Sunshine Way in Distant City, you will note that the contract did not include fencing. If you wish me to have the redwood fence installed, as you requested in your letter of April 4th, I shall be happy to take care of it, but there will be an extra charge of approximately $700.

Please let me know definitely what you decide. If you do want me to contract for the fencing, I will ask for bids and then let you know the exact amount of extra cost involved.

The work is coming along nicely on your duplex, and if the rains hold off I think we may finish slightly ahead of schedule. It will be a handsome property.

Yours very truly,

Richard Roe & Sons

The writer of the above letter finishes on an optimistic note to relieve the unpleasant news in the first paragraph. He succeeds in giving the letter a friendly tone.

Some Everyday Business Refusals

#130 (Letterhead)

October 3, 19___

Mrs. Henry Johnson
232 Pleasant St.
Anytown, N.M. 00000

Dear Mrs. Johnson:

We appreciate your order of September 25th, but we cannot send the merchandise C.O.D., as this is against General Mail Order Co.'s policy. We have found that the added cost and red tape involved in C.O.D. orders amount to such a figure that it would force us to raise the prices on all our merchandise. We believe that most of our customers would prefer to have us keep prices down and sacrifice the slight convenience of the C.O.D. service.

We will be happy to charge the merchandise on any standard bank credit card you may have, if you will send us the number. Or you may, if you wish, send us your check for $37.50, which includes cost of shipping and handling. Please let us know which you prefer by filling out the form at the bottom of this letter and returning it to us in the self-addressed envelope that is enclosed. For your convenience in making future purchases, we have also enclosed a charge account application.

We look forward to serving you.

                                        Sincerely,

                                        George Smith, Director
                                        Customer Relations

Enclosures

_____ Please charge the merchandise   _____ My check to cover the mer-
         referred to. My bank credit   chandise referred to is en-
         card number is: closed.

_____ .

Signature_____

_____

_____

#131   (Letterhead)

                                                              August 14, 19___

Mrs. John Smith
22 Prosperous Lane
Suburbanville, La. 00000

Dear Madam:

We regret to say that we are not equipped to send samples of the merchandise shown in our catalog. We do, however, offer a thirty-day money-back guarantee if merchandise is returned to us in perfect condition. You can thus be assured of complete satisfaction, since you can examine the merchandise itself at your leisure. We think you will be happier in the long run with this arrangement. May we have your order? An order blank and self-addressed envelope are enclosed for your convenience. We accept all standard bank credit cards. Thank you.

Very truly yours,

JOHN DOE MERCHANDISERS

Enclosures

#132   (Letterhead)

March 3, 19____

Mr. John Doe
1012 Broad St.
Anytown, Tenn. 00000

Dear Mr. Doe:

We cannot make a refund of the purchase price on the upholstery fabric you returned to us, as the fabric is water-spotted and soiled in some areas. We can either return the fabric to you or allow you 50% of the original price, to be applied against another purchase.
Please let us know which arrangement you would prefer.

Sincerely,

Customer Service Dept.

#133   (Letterhead)

January 3, 19____

Mr. Robert Smith
9472 Broad St.
Bigtown, Pa. 00000

Dear Mr. Smith:

Since the merchandise you returned to us was purchased more than six weeks ago, we regret to say that our 30-day money-back guarantee has expired. However, because we value your patronage, we will allow you to exchange the watchband for any other merchandise of the same value which we carry; or you may apply the price toward the purchase of a more expensive item.

Please let us have your instructions.

> Yours very truly,
>
> Adjustment Dept.

#134   (Letterhead)

> October 15, 19___

Mrs. Henry Jones
147 Pleasant St.
Suburbanville, Ga. 00000

Dear Mrs. Jones:

We do appreciate the size of the order you are considering sending us, but we regret to say that we cannot sell this merchandise below the price stated in our advertising. The prices shown are rock bottom for this quality, and we do not believe that a better value is obtainable anywhere, if you compare the merchandise for workmanship and material. As we state in our ad in Eminent Magazine, these items have already been reduced $3.00 each, so that on your order for 100 you will be saving $300. You will like our prompt service, also. Your order will be shipped out the same day it is received. I hope that we may serve you.

> Sincerely,
>
> Richard Roe Jewelers

A Refusal to Join in a Business Venture

#135 (Letterhead)

September 3, 19___

Mr. J.B. Venturesome
3012 North St.
Anytown, N. J. 00000

Dear Mr. Venturesome:

Thank you for sending me the information on your real estate trust deal in Delaware. It was interesting, but I am afraid I am going to have to turn down the opportunity because of other commitments. I must admit also that I am always a bit leery of getting myself involved in something that is entirely out of my line. By this I mean that I would want to become thoroughly knowledgeable about any other business and be actively concerned in it were I to consider investing in it. This is no reflection on you or your proposition. It would apply to anything. And as you know, our restaurant business demands absolutely all of my time during this period of expansion.

I am returning your material under separate cover. Again let me thank you for offering to let me share in your venture. I have no doubt you will find plenty of capital and will be successful.

With best personal regards,

John L. Onetrack

The above letter indicates that the writer is fairly well acquainted with Mr. Venturesome and does not wish to offend him. He may have to deal with Venturesome in some other connection.

Refusing to Join an Association

#136   (Letterhead)

April 7, 19___

Mr. John Doe
Reliable Shoe Co.
1011 Business St.
Anytown, Ky. 00000

Dear Mr. Doe:

Our company is a member of the Chamber of Commerce and our Advertising Manager is a member of the City Advertising Club. We feel that these two organizations keep us in touch with general business trends in the city and give us sufficient opportunity to work with other businesses for the common good. Your Neighborhood Merchants Organization may be a good thing for the small businesses on the street—no doubt it is—but it represents a duplication of aims as far as we are concerned.

Smith & Jones certainly wishes you well, however; and we might subscribe to a minimum non-active membership, if this is satisfactory to your other members. We should also be happy to cooperate with you on certain neighborhood promotions, such as moonlight sales, when they do not conflict with our own seasonal plan or our policy.

Cordially,

Richard Roe, Gen. Mgr.

#137   (Letterhead)

April 8, 19___

Mr. John Doe
Reliable Shoe Co.
1011 Business St.
Anytown, Ky. 00000

Dear Mr. Doe:

I thought over the matter of the Neighborhood Merchants Organization that you discussed with me, and I have decided against it. It has been my observation that these groups take up a great deal of time and seldom accomplish very much. In my own case, I simply cannot afford to be away from my store for the meetings, as lunch hours are often our busiest periods.

A year or two from now the situation may change, and I might consider joining then if the organization is still in existence. Thanks for consulting me, in any case.

With best regards,

Henry Johnson

#138 (Letterhead)

June 14, 19___

Mr. Robert Smith
Richard Roe Co.
1011 Busy St.
Bigtown, Ala. 00000

Dear Mr. Smith:

Thank you for your invitation to join your group, but it is against the policy of Giant Corp. to become affiliated with small, specialized associations of this type. Giant stores try instead to identify with, and serve, the entire city.

Yours very truly,

John Doe, Mgr.

Refusing to Give to a Charity

#139   (Letterhead)

February 19, 19___

Mrs. J.L. Socialite
2047 Opulent Lane
Suburbia, W.Va. 00000

Dear Madam:

We regret that we will be unable to contribute to your special charity fund, but it is against the policy of the company. Because of the many appeals, it is company policy to limit our contributions to one large donation to The Community Chest. In this way we hope to cover a great many organizations for the needy, without showing favoritism. We hope you will understand and forgive us.

Yours very truly,

John Doe, Vice Pres.

Refusal to Attend a Meeting

#140   (Letterhead)

August 4, 19___

Mr. John Doe, Secretary
Local Business Men's Assoc.
1719 Main St.
Anytown, Neb. 00000

Dear Mr. Doe:

I am sorry, but because of prior commitments I will be unable to attend the meeting you have arranged for August 15th to discuss the parking problem in the downtown area. Whatever decision you arrive at will in all probability be agreeable to us, because our private parking area pretty well takes care of the parking situation so far as we are concerned. I do appreciate your invitation, however.

Yours very truly,

Richard Roe

Refusal to Give a Job to Someone Recommended to You

#141 (Letterhead)

March 3, 19____

Mr. Richard Roe
Roe Corp.
2047 Broad St.
Bigtown, Conn. 00000

Dear Mr. Roe:

I had an interesting interview with John Doe, the young man you recommended to me. I was impressed with his intelligence and personality; however, I don't think he has had heavy enough experience for the particular post we were discussing. I intend to keep him in mind, though, in case a more suitable opening does occur.

Cordially,

Henry Smith

Refusal to Give a Job to Someone Who Has Applied

A few companies do not bother to inform a job applicant when he has been turned down. It is much more courteous and considerate to let the applicant know, and as soon as possible, even if the briefest form letter is used. The text can read simply, "The position for which you have applied has already been filled. We will keep your application on file, in case another opening does occur." Regarding a more important job, a more elaborate letter may be in order.

#142   (Letterhead)

September 11, 19___

Mr. Richard Roe, Comptroller
Important Corporation
2033 Industrial Road
Eastern City, Mass. 00000

Dear Mr. Roe:

We have carefully considered your credentials and have been favorably
impressed. However, the management felt that it would be wiser to select a
man whose experience more closely parallels the situation in our own
industry. A decision has been made on that basis. Your inquiry will, of
course, be kept confidential.

Yours very truly,

Charles Johnson, Vice Pres.

Refusal to Give a Letter of Recommendation

#143   (Letterhead)

February 4, 19___

Mr. George Smith
1137 Residential St.
Pleasant City, Maine 00000

Dear George:

I regret it very much, but I will be unable to give you the letter of
recommendation you requested. It is a longtime policy of this company
not to furnish such letters. I can assure you, however, that if any inquiries

are made of us we will reply favorably. I personally want to wish you the best of luck. Please keep in touch.

Sincerely,

John Doe

Refusal to Extend Time on a Debt

#144   (Letterhead)

September 11, 19___

Mr. John Doe, President
John Doe Industries
2012 Industrial St.
Anytown, O. 00000

Dear Mr. Doe:

We have carefully gone over the figures that you and Mr. Roe presented last week and we are not optimistic about the picture they present. We do not believe that it would be good business for either the bank or your company for you to be granted an extension on your loan. If you would care to discuss our analysis, our Mr. Jones and I will be glad to go over it with you. Please write or telephone me for an appointment. It is just possible that our analysis might help you to arrive at some other solution to your current problems.

Cordially,

Robert Smith
Loan Officer

#145   (Letterhead)

March 3, 19____

Mr. Joseph Johnson
Blank & Co.
1517 Business St.
Anytown, Montana 00000

Dear Mr. Johnson:

We regret to inform you that current conditions do not warrant our granting an extension on your loan. I hope, however, that you will find another solution to your problems.

Yours very truly,

Robert Smith
Loan Officer

#146   (Letterhead)

June 3, 19____

Mr. John Doe
John Doe Industries
2012 Industrial St.
Anytown, O. 00000

Re: Invoice 319270498

Dear Mr. Doe:

I am sorry, but we cannot extend any more time for payment of the above invoice on machine tools. You must admit that we have been very patient; but if payment in full is not received in this office on or before July 15, 19____, we shall be forced to take legal action.

Yours very truly,

Richard Roe, Supervisor
Accounts Receivable

Refusing to Raise the Budget Limit

#147 (Letterhead)

April 19, 19___

Mr. David Smith, Mgr.
Printing Division
Anonymous Industries
1719 Broad St.
Bigtown, Pa.

Re: Purchase of Graham Collator

Dear Smith:

The Board has thoroughly discussed your request for permission to purchase the Graham Collator, but we feel that this purchase would not be wise during this fiscal year. Although your presentation was impressive and we know there would be many advantages, such a purchase would require raising the budget limit. Both the Board and the Comptroller are opposed to this.

With best personal regards,

George Jones, Vice Pres.

Refusing to Reduce Tenant's Rent

#148 (Letterhead)

January 15, 19___

Mr. Joseph Jones
2047 City St.
Anytown, Del. 00000

Dear Mr. Jones:

We are sorry, but we will be unable to accede to your request for a reduction on the rent for the space you occupy at 2047 City Street. This is a very desirable location, and our rates compare favorably with rates for other space in the area. As a matter of fact, we have a waiting list of applicants for space in that particular building.

I do want to say that we consider you an excellent tenant, and we hope that you will remain with us.

Yours very truly,

John Doe
Real Estate Mgt. Group

Refusing to Give a Raise in Pay

#149   (Letterhead)

September 3, 19___

Mr. Richard Roe, Asst. Regional Mgr.
Miscellaneous Products Co.
910 Wide St.
Anytown, Tenn. 00000

Dear Roe:

Although the company appreciates the fact that you have been with us for nearly a year now, and that your service has been satisfactory, we do not believe that a raise is in order at this time. It is customary for all salaries to be reviewed in February, at the beginning of the new fiscal year. It is possible that you might be considered for a salary increase then, if conditions warrant, and if the figures for your region show substantial improvement.

With best personal regards,

Harry Green
RECRUITMENT & PERSONNEL

The following two letters were written to employees whom the employers were anxious to appease, even though the salary increases were refused.

#150 (Letterhead)

December 3, 19___

Ms. Doris Brown
P.O. Box 0000
Los Angeles, Calif. 00000

Dear Ms. Brown:

I agree that the sales figures for California have improved spectacularly in the last three months, and that a great deal of it may be due to your demonstration tour; but after all, that is why your job was created. We expected these results, because our product is one that needs a personal demonstration. It is too early in the game, however, to begin talking about success. It is important to know whether the tours are a long-term answer to our problem, and whether repeat orders will justify the expense of the tours. Please hang in there.

As I explained to you when you came, we must work together to give this company a solid base once more. It will take at least another three months to see whether or not we have achieved this. If we have, we will be ready then to discuss salary increases. You can rest assured that if your figures continue to be as good as they are now you will be in line.

Let me know if you need any more supplies. Be sure to allow sufficient time for the materials to reach you when you choose the city for delivery.

By the way, all that sunshine is a fringe benefit! We have eight inches of snow here, with more on the way, and it is COLD!

With very best regards,

#151   (Letterhead)

August 13, 19___

Mr. George Anderson
Imperial Hotel
1219 Grand St.
Anytown, La. 00000

Dear Anderson:

I have delayed answering your letter of July 20th because I have not yet been able to arrange the salary increase for you. Conditions have to be right for these things, as you know, and it will probably be another two months before I can swing it. I want you to know that I appreciate what you have done in that area, however; and I agree that you deserve to be rewarded.

With very best regards,

CHAPTER 9

Compliments, Commendations,

and Reprimands

Outright compliments and letters of recommendation are a pleasure to write. About the only problem attending them is deciding on the degree of enthusiasm you want to express! In the case of employees you can be guided by the nature of the person to whom you are writing. There may be a few who will go into a slump if complimented too extravagantly, while others need constant encouragement. Sometimes justified compliments can be used to introduce or cushion necessary criticism, as in letters #157 and #167 in this chapter.

Some Complimentary Letters to Employees

#152

May 21, 19___

Mr. Walter Reynolds
4189 Jefferson St.
Anytown, Calif. 00000

Dear Walt:

Well, you have done it again! You have topped everyone in your area with your sales record for April. Congratulations! If you keep going at this rate you will almost certainly be one of the guys who wins a trip to Bermuda. I've got my eye on a nice bon voyage basket for you!

                                        With best regards,

                    (Signed)   Jack

                                  John Doe, Sales Mgr.

#153   *(Letterhead)*

                                                      March 3, 19___

Mr. George Smith
Luxury Hotel
2012 Broad St.
Bigtown, Wash. 00000

Dear Smith:

I want you to know that I was very impressed with the completeness and soundness of the study you made for the relocation of the Bigtown Airport. I have just finished your lengthy but very well organized report. I think you have given our clients more than their money's worth. Please let me know what reactions you get at the meeting on Monday.

                                        Cordially,

                                  Burton Jones, Vice Pres.

#154   (In-house memo)

February 14, 19___

Miss Jane Smith
Accounting Dept.

Dear Miss Smith:

You will be pleased to know that your work so far has been very satisfactory. Your trial period has been completed and your name is now being transferred to the roster of permanent employees. Welcome to the staff!

Sincerely,

Richard Roe
Personnel Director

#155   (Letterhead)

November 3, 19___

Mr. Henry Davis
1714 Wide Street
Suburbanville, Kans. 00000

Dear Mr. Davis:

Your plans for the Suburbanville Shopping Center are a spectacular achievement, in my opinion. If the development company does not approve them forthwith, they should have their heads examined. You have given every little shop its own importance, in spite of there being too many in the plan, and the traffic pattern is great. The sketches and elevations are beautiful, too, as usual.

I will be down on Wednesday to join you in the presentation. The plane gets in at seven, so don't bother to meet me. I will take a cab to your hotel, and perhaps we can have breakfast together. I look forward to seeing you.

Sincerely,

John Smith

#156   (Letterhead)

January 3, 19___

Mr. Jerry Guffey
1217 Suburban St.
Pleasant Town, Ca. 00000

Dear Jerry:

The management is very pleased with your work and I have had nothing but good reports from your customers. Beginning March 1 you will be transferred to a permanent route. Two, and perhaps three, routes will be open at that time, and you may have your choice of them. I shall have more information on this for you within a week or ten days.

With best regards,

John Doe
District Supervisor

In the following letter a compliment is used to soften some criticism.

#157   (Letterhead)

June 9, 19___

Mr. Leo Guerrez
Dynamic Displays
1011 Little Street
Metropolis, N.Y. 00000

Dear Mr. Guerrez:

I have had very good comments on the displays you have created for our suburban stores, and I myself think they are beautiful. There are two points, however, that are causing some difficulty and I wonder if you could do something about them.

Although most of the buyers and department managers praise your work, some of the same ones are complaining that you are turning their departments upside down in the busiest part of the day, and are requiring the assistance of too many salespeople.

I realize that many buyers are not the easiest people in the world to get along with, and that some disruption is necessary, but do you think there is some way you could manage to lessen the confusion on the selling floor? Perhaps you could schedule your work earlier in the day—even before the store opens. And perhaps it would help if all mannequins were dressed in the stockroom. What do you say?

There is another point which I hate to bring up, but it is necessary. As you know, you have been going more and more over the budget for display each month, and this simply cannot continue. I must ask that you pare expenditures by at least 10% for the rest of the year, or I fear we shall have nothing to spend for the Christmas season coming up. I think you will agree with me that would be a disaster.

Again I want to tell you how happy we are with your displays. You are a true artist, and I hope that you will be associated with us for many years to come. I am sure you can work things out to keep both the testy buyers and the budget in equilibrium. Please let me hear from you.

With best personal regards,

Richard Roe
Promotion Manager

Praising a Department or Group

In a letter praising a group it is important to get a spirit of warmth and sincerity, so that each member feels that he shares the praise. In one of the following letters the writer goes to the extent of listing all department members, with very good effect.

#158 (Letterhead)

April 30, 19___

Miss Jenny Bowen, Buyer
Lingerie Dept.
Quality Wares Co.
Prosperous Town, Ill. 00000

Dear Miss Bowen:

All figures are in for the Easter season just past, and Mr. Warren, Mr. Gates and I have been going over them very carefully. All stores and nearly all departments did very well, surpassing association averages, we are happy to say One department, however, did spectacularly well, topping all other departments in its gain over last year's excellent figures.

THAT DEPARTMENT WAS YOURS, Miss Bowen!

I want to congratulate you for the excellent merchandising and management that put your department at the top, but most especially I want to congratulate and thank every member of your department for his or her help in achieving this success.

THANK YOU AND CONGRATULATIONS TO EVERY ONE OF YOU:

Alice Arthur	Walt Donaldson	Bea Kline
Jean Aiken	Maria Dumas	Betty Smith
Caroline Burns	Sarah Levine	Kay Thompson
Harry Byers		Donna Walters

Miss Bowen, please see that every member of your department reads and initials this letter. We are proud of you and of them.

Sincerely,

JOHN DOE
General Manager

#159　　　　　　　　　　(In-house memo)

February 12, 19___

TO; Mr. Robert Brown, Foreman
Shop #5
Outlying City, Mo. 00000

From: H.C. Treadway

Subject: CONGRATULATIONS AND NOTICE OF MEETING

Dear Bob Brown:

Please convey my heartfelt congratulations to all the men and women in Shop No. 5. Congratulations to you, also. Shop No. 5 has won the Safety Trophy for the year with an almost perfect record. We are proud of all of you, and gratified to know that a great deal of human suffering and hardship has been barred out by your carefulness and alertness. That you did this while increasing production makes your record that much more commendable.

<u>PLEASE CALL A MEETING FOR WEDNESDAY, FEBRUARY 15TH</u>

<u>10 A.M. IN YOUR LOCAL MEETING ROOM</u>

All Personnel Is
Asked to Attend

I personally hope to present the Safety Trophy to Shop No. 5 at this meeting, as well as the individual awards. In case I cannot be there, Mr. J.J. Pierson will do the honors. Please see that breakfast refreshments are provided for everyone.

H.C. Treadway, President

A Letter Commending an Associate

#160   **(Letterhead)**

June 11, 19___

Mr. Walter Green, Vice Pres.
Corp. Planning & Marketing
New Publishing Corp.
Big City, Ill. 00000

Dear Green:

I felt that I just had to write you and tell you how impressed I was with your speech to the publishers' group. I am sure that many news organizations will be better run as a result of your exposition. I know that I myself have a better understanding of the detailed analysis and imaginative planning that have contributed so much to our stable position. I wanted to tell you this at the time, but you were surrounded with questioners − naturally.

With warmest regards,

A Commendation of a Company the Writer Deals With

#161   (Letterhead)

April 10, 19___

Mr. Howard Jones, President
Quality Printers
3912 Broad St.
Anytown, Miss. 00000

Dear Howard:

Today I went down to your plant, as I have so many times in the past, to confer about a tentative project. I came away with all the information I needed, all the facts and figures, as well as some good advice. More than this, and perhaps more important, I came away with a warm glow and with added zest for my job. I thought you would like to know about this.

I find it a real pleasure to work with your people. Everyone—the telephone operators, the desk clerks, the pressmen—and of course Bill Greenburg—really seems to go out of his way to show concern and to be helpful.

Like everyone else, I am always ready to criticize or show annoyance when things do not please me. Today I just thought I would take a minute to express appreciation for one of the pleasures I have encountered.

Yours very truly,

Hank White

Commending an Accepted Idea

#162   (Letterhead)

June 23, 19____

Mr. Henry Smith
Solid Products Div.
Adhesive Products
7092 Distant Lane
Port City, N.J. 00000

Dear Mr. Smith:

Mr. Jones, the Promotion Director, tells me you are the person who first suggested that we modernize some of our package designs. Good for you! I believe your idea will be of real benefit to the company, and I have submitted your name with a recommendation to the Awards Committee. On behalf of the company, I wish to thank you.

Sincerely,

John Doe, President

#163   (Letterhead)

March 3, 19____

Mr. George Clark
Similar Company
912 Distant Road
Industrial Settlement, Ind. 00000

Dear George:

The suggestion you made to me concerning the re-routing of work order parts is positively brilliant. The more I think of it, the better it looks, and I want to thank you. Perhaps we should have lunch together more often!

With very best regards,

(Signed)   Harry

P.S. How about next Thursday for lunch at the Embassy Club? One o'clock?

#164   (In-house memo)

August 5, 19___

To: Donald Smith, Sales Dept.
From: Harry Jackson

I think your idea about revising the format of the Employee's Manual is excellent. I will use some of your other thoughts, also. Any time you have a suggestion on something like this—any company practices—please send it along. Working together in this way benefits all of us.

(Signed) H.J.

Complimenting a Proffered Idea You Cannot Use

In turning down ideas or suggestions that are intended to be helpful, most good executives take care to be very diplomatic, not wanting to discourage the employee who is interested in the company's general well-being. There is always the chance, too, that the idea which follows an impractical one may turn out to be immensely helpful. Here are texts that could be used in letters or memos:

#165   (Use appropriate stationery)

(a) Thank you for your interesting suggestion about increasing the number of our deliveries. I should very much like to follow through on it, but I'm afraid the expense would be prohibitive at the present time.

(b) Your suggestion about revising the format of the Employee Manual is a good one. I shall keep it on file and give it careful consideration the next time the manual is scheduled for revision—possibly next year.

(c) I appreciate your suggestions concerning our advertising. You can be sure they will be discussed and given much thought at our coming meetings. We consider the input from interested employees very important.

(d) Your idea that we should invade the foreign market is an interesting one, even though the financial picture is not right for it at this time. We shall certainly keep your suggestion in mind for possible future development. Thank you for your concern.

There are times when you must tread very carefully in refusing a suggestion. The following model letter has extraordinary warmth and consideration.

#166   (In-house memo)

November 22, 19___

TO: Benjamin Ames, Mgr.
      Dept. 420

FROM: Edwin Jones

Dear Ben:

That was certainly an ingenious idea you sent me, and your presentation was excellent. I only wish we could use it; however, I am afraid the cost is far beyond anything we had envisioned. I have had to settle for something much more modest.

Thank you for your efforts, anyhow. I hope I can call on you again. We need imagination like yours.

(Signed) Ed

Letters of Reprimand or Criticism

In composing letters of reprimand or criticism make sure that anger is not exaggerating the offense that you object to. It is usually best to adopt a judicial tone. If you have any doubt as to your objectivity, save your letter for several days and then re-read it. Most of the letters given here are fairly mild, yet effective.

Letters Reprimanding a Single Employee, a Group

#167   (Letterhead)

May 15, 19___

Mr. Richard Roe
Versatile Industries
1932 Business St.
Central City, Ga. 00000

Dear Roe:

I have received a complaint from the purchasing agent of Retail Converters Co. stating that you used insulting language toward him when you were requested to straighten out a mix-up in an order. It is his belief that the mix up was your fault, but this is beside the point.

Good customer relations is an ironclad policy of our company, no matter what the situation. I personally believe that anything which needs to be said can be said courteously, even diplomatically. By apparently not following this rule you have endangered our relationship with a possible long-term customer.

In an attempt to make amends, I have now straightened out the situation concerning the order, even though it caused us to take a slight loss. I now request that you write or see Mr. Robert Smith of Retail Converters and apologize for having upset him by losing your temper. It is absolutely necessary that you re-establish a good relationship with this company. Now that you have calmed down and Mr. Smith has been somewhat appeased, I am sure that your demonstrated talents as a good salesman will enable you to do this.

Yours very truly,

John Doe, Gen. Mgr.

#168   (Letterhead)

October 3, 19___

Mr. Henry Nemo, Dept. Mgr.
Paper Goods and Wrapping
Anonymous Industries, Plant 3
Outlying City, Or. 00000

    Re: Fire Insurance Increase

Dear Mr. Nemo:

I have received notification from Fire Insurance Underwriters that our insurance on Plant 3 will be increased by 40% for the coming year. Upon inquiry, I was told that unsafe and even illegal conditions have been allowed to exist in your department, and that this is the cause of the increase. I double-checked and found that you have had two citations from your area's Fire Marshall for the same conditions during the last six months.

I am astounded that you would allow this threat to life and property to exist, especially when you have been warned. I insist that you acquaint yourself with the regulations and clear up this dangerous situation forthwith. If new containers are required, send me your order immediately and I will okay it. I want to see a safety certification from your local Fire Inspector within twenty-one days from the date of this letter.

                  Yours very truly,

                  Jane Doe, Vice Pres.
                  Paper Goods & Wrapping Div.

#169   (Letterhead)

May 23, 19___

Mr. James Jackson
Oldline Corporation
191 Broad St.
Pequeno, Ca. 00000

Dear Jackson:

The enclosed notice is being sent to all employees who attended the regional meeting at Laguna last week. You are requested to call a departmental meeting at the earliest opportunity and to read this notice to your people. I consider this matter extremely important, and your cooperation will be appreciated.

Yours very truly,

Richard Roe, President

Enc.

AN IMPORTANT NOTICE
TO ALL EMPLOYEES OF
OLDLINE CORPORATION

From President Richard Roe

The president of your company was distressed, I might even say outraged, at the behavior of many Oldline employees who attended the meeting in the amphitheater at Laguna. The discourtesy shown our guest speaker was unforgivable. I refer to those who talked during the speech, and most especially to those who had the effrontery to leave the stands before the speech was completed. I should like to remind you that you were on the payroll of this company at that time, and simple honesty, if not ordinary courtesy, should have kept you in respectful attendance.

I consider it unfortunate that the management did not anticipate such ill-mannered behavior, otherwise disciplinary action would be taken against offenders. Many are known, of course, but not all. To each and every one of you, known and unknown, I want to say that such behavior will not be tolerated on any future occasion of this sort.

This is a message I never imagined I should have to deliver to our people. I hope now that it was only the informal atmosphere of the beach city that caused you to forget your manners in this embarrassing way. I hope and trust that I may never again be forced to send such a message to you.

Signed: Richard Roe, President

Letters of Recommendation, References

Some large companies make it a rule not to give explicit references for past employees, using a simple form as a reply to all inquiries. An example:

#170   (Letterhead)

(Date)

To:

Re: Employment Record

Dear Sir or Madam:

It is against the policy of this company to go into a detailed discussion of past employees' performance while here. Our records show that
Name _____
was employed by us from _____ to _____.

BLANK & CO.

One such company I knew had a personnel clerk write "Services satisfactory" across the bottom of the card, if this were true. Otherwise there was no comment. (A red check mark on the past employee's file card was a signal to the clerk to omit the comment.)

Regardless of such procedures and total company policy, the individual employer or department head may wish to give a more detailed reference, or even a letter of recommendation, to someone who has performed well. The following such letters show varying degrees of enthusiasm and endorsement. Choose the type best suited to your purpose.

#171   **(Letterhead)**

August 14, 19___

Mr. Hugh Roberts, Traffic Mgr.
General Manufacturing Co.
2010 Industrial Road
Anytown, Idaho 00000

Dear Mr. Roberts:

I am happy to recommend Alice Blanton. She is proficient in secretarial
skills, intelligent, dependable, and well organized. Miss Blanton also has
the rather rare ability to compose the bulk of routine letters when she is
given a sketchy summary of what is wanted.

Yours very truly,

John Doe, Gen. Mgr.

#172   **(Letterhead)**

March 3, 19___

Mr. Howard Barnes, Supervisor
Drafting Division
Leading Construction Co., Inc.
Anytown, Mont. 00000

Dear Mr. Barnes:

I can heartily recommend the services of John Campo, who worked as
draftsman in my department for a number of years. He is accurate, fast,
and dependable, and can work with the minimum of direction. He is also a
very likable person.

Yours very truly,

Richard Roe, Vice Pres.

#173　　　　　　　　(Letterhead)

Sept. 19, 19___

Mr. Paul McNamara, Supervisor
Manuals Division
Giant Industrial Co.
Outlying Town, Mass. 00000

Dear Mr. McNamara:

I am happy to recommend Mr. Harry Godowski as a technical writer. He writes with clarity and skill, yet his instructions are often surprisingly brief. Mr. Godowski is conversant with Milspecs and is very good at interpreting blueprints and engineering drawings. At the same time this writer can be depended upon to go to the source and investigate any angle that may need clarification. We found Mr. Godowski's services more than satisfactory.

Yours very truly,

John Doe, Mgr.
Technical Writing Div.

#174　　　　　　　　(Letterhead)

January 24, 19___

Mr. Ben Greenburg, Pres.
Communications Co.
1915 Broad St.
Bigtown, Md. 00000

Dear Mr. Greenburg:

Mr. Howard James' record with our company was excellent. He is a fine administrator, has a creative mind, and is able to secure the enthusiastic cooperation of those who work with him or under him.

Very truly yours,

Richard Roe, Vice Pres.

#175   (Letterhead)

November 3, 19____

Mr. George Hendrix, Mgr.
Shipping Dept.
General Manufacturing Co.
Anytown, S.D. 00000

Dear Mr. Hendrix:

Robert Baumann is a good, dependable worker who does his job effi-
ciently and gets along well with his associates. I believe he will be an asset
to any company with which he is connected.

Sincerely,

Richard Roe
CHIEF SHIPPING CLERK

Any of the above letters of recommendation, which were
written in reply to inquiries, can be adapted as letters of introduction
with minor changes. An added first paragraph might read:

This is to introduce _____ who
worked with me (or for me) at Blank Corp. for a number of years.

Another first paragraph might read:

This letter will recommend _____
with whom I was associated at Blank Corp. for many years.

Letters of Introduction

Some letters of introduction or recommendation that are to be
presented to many different persons are headed To Whom It May
Concern:. This heading should be avoided if possible because it is too
general and is often used to introduce an unpleasant notice. Choose a
more specific salutation, if you can. The following are good:

(1) TO PROSPECTIVE EMPLOYERS:

(2) INTRODUCING MR. RICHARD ROE.

(3) A RECOMENDATION OF MISS JANE DOE.

Under such a heading you may begin your letter with the customary "Dear Sir:", if you wish, or omit it and go right into your message.

A Letter Introducing One Friend of Yours to Another

#176 (Letterhead)

July 12, 19___

Mr. Henry Brown
Important Brokerage Co.
912 Financial St.
Metropolis, N.Y. 00000

Dear Brown:

This will introduce Mr. Alan G. Jones, a good friend of mine who was associated with me for many years at Blank & Co. Originally a Chicagoan, he is locating in New York for the first time. I will appreciate anything you can do to make his stay more pleasant. (*Or* his introduction to your city more pleasant.)

I think you and Al will find quite a few things to talk about. Like you, he is a low 80's golfer, and he is also an avid stamp collector. I have told him about your huge collection and he is anxious to see it.

Very best regards to you, Harry. I am hoping that I, myself, will get to New York some time in October, and I shall look forward to seeing both of you fellows then. In the meantime, write me.

Sincerely,

Richard Roe

In any personal introduction like the foregoing it is important to tell something about the person you are introducing, so that the two being brought together will have something to talk about when they meet.

Negative Replies to Requests for References

Because of legal angles, if not humane considerations, writing a negative reply to a request for references is something that should be given a great deal of thought. If you feel you must condemn a past employee, mild generalities will serve as well as an angry blast. The following phrases are examples of this technique, and are quite sufficient without any further remarks. Use them in the standard letter form.

#177   (Letterhead)

(a) In regard to your inquiry about Jane Doe, I can only say that she was not one of the best of our employees.

(b) We found that Richard Roe needed constant supervision.

(c) In regard to your inquiry about John Doe, I can only say that we were not happy about our association with this employee.

CHAPTER 10

Letters Concerning Credit, Price

Changes, Customer Complaints

Letters in this chapter cover a wide range of skills in letter-writing. Many of them, surprisingly enough, are sales letters, as will be pointed out.

Letters Offering to Open an Account

Letters offering to open an account are actually sales letters. They should sell the advantages of credit, and the advantages of dealing with your particular company. Some such letters may enclose a credit card, if legal considerations have been taken into account and proper investigations made. Others will enclose a pared-down credit application. Some examples follow:

#178   (Letterhead)

October 3, 19___

Mr. and Mrs. James Rockford
1011 Prestigious St.
Bigtown, Ma. 00000

Dear Mr. and Mrs. Rockford:

We know you will be delighted to hear that a new Smith & Co. store will
be opening next month in the shopping center in your area. Within
minutes of your home, all the quality products and services for which
Smith & Co. is famous will now be available:

Ladies' Apparel and Accessories		Men's Wear and Men's Furnishings
Cosmetics	Lingerie	Infants' and Children's Wear
Hosiery	Foundations	Housewares and Appliances
Robes	Jewelry	

So that you can share in all the opening-day specials, including many for
charge customers only, we are enclosing a Smith & Co. charge card made
out in your name. All you need do is sign it on the back and present it
when you wish to make a purchase. It is good at all Smith & Co. stores, of
course. A booklet covering details is closed.

We will send you notice soon of the exact date of the store opening in
your area, together with news of the exciting sale features. In the
meantime your account is already open. You may use it imediately!

Yours very truly,

Richard Roe, President

Enc.

#179   (Letterhead)

March 31, 19____

Ms. Theresa Goldberg, Manager
Supply Dept.
Eminent Manufacturing Co.
220 Broad St.
Anytown, Ind. 00000

Dear Ms. Goldberg:

We'd like to bring to your attention two important services that make
Quality Stationers the preferred suppliers for many leading businesses in
Anytown.

1. Your Credit is Good at Quality Stationers

    No forms to fill out. A 30-day account is established automat-
    ically with your first order. Terms 2% 10 days.

2. We Deliver

    Same day delivery on many orders, saving you time and the
    expense of sending your own messenger. Check on the delivery
    date when you place your order.

Please take a minute now to try us out. What do you need? Business
forms? Envelopes? Copier paper? Whatever it is, telephone 234-7900.
You'll be glad you did.

Yours very truly,

George Blank, Gen. Mgr.

P.S. Write our telephone number down for future use. It's 234-7900.
Better yet, slip the enclosed card under the glass on your desk.

(Hand-initialed) G.B.

#180   (Letterhead)

February 23, 19___

Mrs. G. Carlton Hendrix
7942 Posh Boulevard
Suburbanville, Tenn. 00000

Dear Madam:

With the approach of the joyous season of weddings and graduations you will find a charge account at Eminent Jewelers & Silversmiths a tremendous convenience. Much of your important gift shopping can be done over the telephone, saving you time when time is at a premium You can be sure that the gifts you order will express the utmost in good taste and will be of outstanding quality. Each will be delivered, gift-wrapped, and with your card enclosed, by Eminent's uniformed messenger.

Won't you take a moment now to fill out the enclosed Account Request card? Just mail it back to us in the enclosed postage-paid envelope. Within a few days, when credit is approved, your Charge Plate will arrive.

Eminent Jewelers & Silversmiths looks forward to serving you.

Respectfully,

(Signed)   John Doe

For EMINENT JEWELERS
& SILVERSMITHS

Enc.

Letters Offering Extra Christmas Credit

"Buy now, pay in February," is usually the message these letters carry. Some letters enclose scrip issued by the merchant and labeled *Holiday Money*. Others enclose holly-printed stickers or Santa Claus stickers to be applied to pre-holiday saleschecks to signal that payment is to be deferred.

Be sure your letter describes your offer fully. If no interest is to be charged until February 1, be sure to say so, as this is a big selling point. On the other hand, if interest begins at date of purchase, the law in most states requires that this be mentioned in the letter and on the scrip itself.

To emphasize the holiday atmosphere you may want to use a special letterhead, and perhaps print your message in green.

Here is a sample letter:

#181   **(Letterhead)**

October 10, 19___

Mrs. J.W. Smith
1011 Residential St.
Anytown, Nev. 00000

Dear Charge Customer:

Santa's on his way and we are ready for him with a giant Pre-Holiday Sale, beginning Thursday, October 23rd! To help you take advantage of the bargains, and to spread your holiday purchases over a longer period, we are enclosing $250 of HOLIDAY MONEY for you.

<u>Spend Your Holiday Money Like Cash in Any Department—</u>

<u>Make No Payment Until February 1 of Next Year!</u>

You may pay in February and there will be no finance charge at all. Or you may spread your payments over many months at the usual revolving charge account rate. Interest charges do not begin until February, in this case. (See reverse side of Holiday Money for details.)

It's the happiest way to do Christmas shopping. Make your gift list now and be ready to reap the savings in the Pre-Holiday Sale. Holiday Money will make your shopping fast and easy. Merry Christmas!

Sincerely,

Richard Roe, President

P.S. Your HOLIDAY MONEY may be used now, on anything we sell, and through the Holiday Season . . . Until January 31st next year.

Letters Announcing a Rise in Prices

In most such letters you take the sting out of the price rise by giving the customer the opportunity to stock up at the old price. An example:

#182 (Letterhead)

July 15, 19___

Mr. Jacob Bernstein
Bernstein Brothers
937 Busy St.
Anytown, Ala. 00000

Dear Mr. Bernstein:

In making plans for fall we find that the rising cost of materials will make it necessary to raise prices by 10% on our entire Broadway line. We are happy to say, however, that we have a large inventory of these items as of now. We are suggesting to our regular customers that they order now, anticipating later needs, to avoid the price rise. Once our stock on hand is depleted there will be no more of this merchandise at today's prices. Please let me hear from you at your earliest convenience.

You may order now for delivery any time before October 15th.

Sincerely,

(Signed)   Sam

Sam Bloom
John Doe Industries

Letters Aimed at Reviving Inactive Accounts

Once again, when you are seeking to regain a lost customer, your letter must do a selling job. If possible, offer something new or at least give some news that will excite interest. Make your letter subtly flattering, even apologetic, and have it signed by an officer of the company. Having done all this, make sure you follow up on that letter. Tell your employees about your campaign to regain lost customers and insist they treat all customers with utmost courtesy and consideration. (The customer who was driven away by real or fancied rudeness will be gone forever if she is brushed aside when she returns.)

Here are some model letters you can revise slightly to fit your situation:

#183   (Letterhead)

March 15, 19___

Mrs. H.V. Opulent
3019 Prosperous Way
Suburbanville, Idaho 00000

Dear Mrs. Opulent:

Was it our fault? Did one of us do something that displeased you?

If this is why you no longer come to our store in Big City, I wish that you would tell me about it and give me the opportunity to right the wrong. You can do this by sending me a note or by telephoning me at 000-3492, extension 47. I will be most happy to talk to you personally. I want you to know that John Doe Brothers really means it when we say that the customer is always right.

If, after all, it was nothing that we did that kept you away, but just a change in your routine, John Doe Brothers should very much like to welcome you back. As a special Welcome Back offer we are enclosing a card for you which will give you a special 10% discount on any merchandise you purchase in our store from March 17th until the end of April, 19___. Please use your discount card and enjoy it. Just present it with your charge plate. We think you will be delighted with the new apparel we are showing now in our fashion boutiques on the second floor.

Sincerely,

John Doe, President

Enc.

#184   (Letterhead)

March 3, 19___

Mrs. H.V. Opulent
3019 Prosperous Way
Suburbanville, Idaho 00000

Dear Mrs. Opulent:

Don't mislay the enclosed card. It is our special invitation to you to attend
the preview of our new enlarged nursery section next Monday—and it
entitles you to a FREE BABY ORCHID CORSAGE!

Just Present The Card to The Plant Expert
Who Greets You, Any Time Between 10 and 5,
Monday, March 10th
And He Will Pin On Your Orchid Corsage

No purchase is required. We just want you to see the tremendous display
of flowers, ornamentals, fruit trees and shrubs we have collected for Idaho
gardeners. There will be specials, of course, for those who are already
planning their gardens or landscaping; but no one will urge you to buy. It's
a party! Just come in, and see, and sniff, and enjoy!

Sincerely,

Richard Roe, President
Fabulous Flower Shoppe

#185   (Letterhead)

September 2, 19___

Mr. John Affluent
1020 Prestige Rd.
Suburbia, Ma. 00000

Dear Mr. Affluent:

We've missed you. Won't you please tell us what it is that has kept you
away? If you think we should make amends for some failing, we will
certainly try, because we value your good will.

The enclosed card is offered for your comments. If you will please fill it in and mail it back to me in the postage-paid envelope, I will give it my personal attention.

Respectfully,

Richard Roe, Manager

P.S. Our new Harris Tweeds have arrived. They still have the smell of peat about them—and they are specially priced during September.

(Initialed)   R.R.

Collection Letters

Most businesses strive to project a friendly, attractive image to the public and to their customers. It is considered so important that some giant corporations expend millions of dollars on advertising and public relations budgets. Unfortunately, in some organizations, the roles of the accounting and credit departments in regard to this image are overlooked. Terse, even rude, letters are sent out by some thoughtless credit personnel, unmindful of the fact that a company error may be involved in the situation. Beware of this failing. Let all your letters, even those aimed at collecting bad debts, be models of courtesy. One tactless letter sent out when you are at fault may lose a very valuable customer.

For longtime customers whose record of payment is very good, wise companies use a very gentle reminder as the first notice of an overdue bill. It is usually a specially printed card that is stapled to the duplicate of the overdue bill. An example:

#186   (Card)

Please—

Our records show that this bill is overdue. If it has not already been paid, please send us your check. Thank you.

EMINENT JEWELERS

For the bulk of overdue accounts a series of form letters serves very well. The first reminder can be a duplicate bill stamped in red as overdue. Something like this is effective: <u>YOUR BILL IS OVER-</u> <u>DUE. Have you forgotten? Please send your check today.</u> (This is step 1 in the collection series.)

Steps 2, 3, and 4 are letters of increasing insistence. Here are examples:

Step 2.   #187 (Letterhead or card enclosed with bill)

January 29, 19___

Mr. John Doe
2440 Blank Ave.
Anytown, N.M. 00000

A REMINDER–

Perhaps you have overlooked it, but your account with us is overdue. Please send us your check in the amount of _____ for purchases as shown on the enclosed statement. An envelope addressed to us is enclosed. Thank you.

(Signed) Betty Martin

Collection Dept.
Richard Roe & Co.

Step 3.   #188   (Letterhead)

February 15, 19___

Mr. John Doe
2440 Blank Ave.
Anytown, N.M. 00000

Dear Sir:

Richard Roe & Co. hates to nag, but you are damaging your excellent credit record with us and costing both of us money, with mounting service charges for you and extra accounting expense for us. Won't you please stop right now and make out your check for the amount due on your account, which is $ _____ . An envelope addressed to us is enclosed.

If for any reason you cannot do this, please telephone your account representative and let us know what the situation is, so that we can, perhaps, delay the reclassification of your account.

Yours very truly,

Your Account Representative
Collection Dept.
Richard Roe & Co.

Step 4.   #189   (Letterhead)

NOTICE OF DELINQUENT ACCOUNT (Stamped or printed in red)

March 15, 19___

Mr. John Doe
2440 Blank Ave.
Anytown, N.M. 00000

Dear Sir:

We tried. We have valued you in the past as a good customer with a fine credit record, but as you know, every company must collect its bills in order to stay in business.

With regret we must now inform you that a time limit has been set for payment of your account, in the amount of $ _____ including service charges, for purchases made _____. If payment is made before _____ you can avoid having your account turned over to a collection agency. Please act now.

Your Account Representative

Collection Department
Richard Roe & Co.

Not all Collection Department situations can be handled by simple form letters. Here are some model letters dealing with more complex situations. Notice the tact and courtesy that characterize them.

#190   (Letterhead)

June 4, 19___

Mr. Richard Roe
1413 Business St.
Bigtown, Mich. 00000

        Re: Invoice #27193259

Dear Mr. Roe:

We have carefully checked our accounts and can find no record of the
payment you believe you made April 2 to cover the sum of $297.48 due
on Invoice #27193259. If you have received your canceled check from the
bank, please send us a photocopy of it so that we can clear up this matter
expeditiously. If you find you were mistaken about the payment, please
send payment immediately. Thank you.

                                    Yours very truly,

                                    Accounting Dept.

#191   (Letterhead)

April 17, 19___

Ms. Jane Doe, Bookkeeping Dept.
General Merchandise Co.
9411 Business St.
Busy Town, Wash. 00000

        Re: Invoice #341182916, March 15, 19___

Dear Ms. Doe:

Thank you for your check in the amount of $319.50, which you had
earmarked as payment for the March 15 invoice noted above. We
appreciate the payment, but it does not cover the full amount due. As you
will note on the copy of the invoice which is enclosed, someone
apparently mistook the SUBTOTAL figure for the amount due. There
remains a balance of $57.00, which is now overdue. Please send us a check
for this amount.

If the error is corrected before April 30, you will not lose the 1% discount. Payment after that date should include $3.76 additional, making the total amount $60.76.

Sincerely,

Accounting Dept.

Enc.

#192 (Letterhead)

August 3, 19____

Mr. Richard Roe
1720 Winding Road
Businesstown, Vt. 00000

Re: Invoice #331219274 dated June 1, 19____

Dear Mr. Roe:

We were wrong, and we wish to apologize. Your account, as you said, is paid in full. Your check for $2019.20 dated June 10 was somehow routed to Plant 12 and was then misdirected to Plant 10, so that we have only now received it. How these errors occur one never knows, but we are taking extra precautions to see that this sort of thing does not happen again. Thank you for your patience and understanding.

Yours very truly,

James Smith, Mgr.
Accounts Receivable

On the bills for revolving credit accounts more explanation is sometimes necessary. One of the large mail order companies sends out a statement with an extra portion attached at the bottom. Under a printed heading, About Your Account . . . , a typewritten message is filled in:

#193   (Statement form with space for message)

Your account is past due $15. If you have not paid this amount, please send it today, together with the current monthly payment which was due upon receipt of your statement.

Amount Past Due: $15   Monthly Payment Rate: $15

Please pay the total now due, which is $30.

(Printed line) IF YOU HAVE ALREADY MADE THIS PAYMENT, PLEASE DISREGARD THIS NOTICE.

Some credits snarls are extremely complicated and should probably be referred to management for a reply as company policy may be involved. The following letter is an example:

#194

March 11, 19___

Mr. John Doe
John Doe & Co.
P.O. Box 000
Anyville, Ark. 00000

      Re: Your Delinquent Account for
            Storage During Longshoremen's Strike

Dear Mr. Doe:

I have checked with the Gulf Port Authority as you requested, to see if some relief was being provided to shippers who were forced to store goods which arrived here during the Longshoremen's Strike. The Authority informs me that the only relief provided at any port in the U.S. is a reduction from the Wharf Demurrage rate to the much lower Wharf Storage rate. A copy of the Authority's reply to my inquiry is attached.

As you know, and as the attached bills and documents show, we have given you this reduced rate from the beginning. (We have done this with all our customers, in a move to share the extra costs caused by the strike.) I am sure you realize also that we could have demanded payment in advance; but during all our years of warehousing, involving millions of bales of cotton, we have never found this to be necessary. Our clients customarily live up to their commitments.

It is unfortunate that shippers incurred extra costs because of the strike, costs that they were unable to plan for in advance, but hardships were suffered by all businesses concerned, including our own. As your bills indicate, our company has already paid on your behalf the charges called for by Tarriff 00, under our agreement to honor all such commitments as a service to the shipper.

Now that you understand the situation, we request that you honor your commitment promptly, so that we can clear our books and get back to the regular order of business.

As shown by the enclosed bills, the total amount now overdue is $2,471.75. Please send your check for that amount.

Very truly yours,

Richard Roe
General Manager

Enc.

In the above letter the emphasis on honoring commitments was deliberate. It reminds the customer that a business such as his can only run smoothly when the parties involved can have faith in each other. The phrase also subtly suggests a legal angle. Naturally, such strong wording would only be used in exceptional cases.

Replying to Customer Complaints

Letters answering customer complaints should take into account the importance of keeping the customer as a patron of your business. The wording depends in some degree on company policy. Many businesses operate on the principle that the customer is always right, which makes replies to complaints quite simple. One department store owner I know goes even further. When faced with an irate customer's complaint, he writes a letter like the following one, and he claims that he has never been embarrassed by the result. "The customer is so startled by our attitude," he says, "that he or she usually demands far less than one would have expected."

A Letter That Goes All the Way

#195   (Letterhead)

January 14, 19___

Mrs. Richard Roe
910 Any Street
Anytown, Ca. 00000

Dear Mrs. Roe:

I was very sorry to hear about the situation that developed concerning the sofa that you purchased at our store, and I apologize for any inconvenience you may have been caused. Please let me know what you think we should do about the sofa. Whatever you think is fair, I personally will see that it is done, and as quickly as possible.

               Sincerely,

               John Doe, President

Few businesses take a chance on going this far to make a complaining customer happy. A series of more usual letters follows, covering a number of situations. The first is a specially-written letter accepting the blame, in an effort to save the relationship with a valuable customer. In this case the company was definitely at fault.

#196   (Letterhead)

August 3, 19___

Mr. Henry Clemens
3709 Any Street
Anytown, Pa. 00000

Dear Mr. Clemens:

I don't blame you for being angry about the outrageous mix-up that developed around your order. Certainly no merchandise should be refused without a double-check down the line. Those of us in charge here stress this in our instructions constantly, yet it seems the element of human error is just bound to creep in on occasion.

All I can say is that I am sorry, and beg you to accept my apology. Of all the people I know, you, who are so careful, are the last one I should want to be inconvenienced in this way.

I have given orders now that whenever there is any question concerning your account in the future that it shall be referred directly to me.

John Doe & Co. value your patronage, and I hope that we can put this thing behind us now and go back to our pleasant and mutually profitable relationship. I expect to be in your city early next month and will stop by. (You can take a punch at me, if you like.) In the meantime, if there is anything I can do to be of service, please telephone me collect.

> With warmest personal regards,
>
> Sales Manager
> John Doe & Co.

#197   **(Form Letter)**

June 7, 19___

Miss Anne Smith
9012 Residential St.
Anytown, O. 00000

Dear Madam:

We apologize for the error that resulted in an overcharge for the merchandise you ordered. The amount due should read $ _____ .
Thank you for calling this to our attention.

> Sincerely,
>
> Jennie Jones
> Customer Service Dept.

If a refund is due the customer, another sentence is typed in at the end: Our check for $ _____ is enclosed.

Multiple Purpose Letters

Some businesses, especially mail order companies, use a form letter like the next one given, to cover many situations. You may use this method if you think it is appropriate. On the other hand, if you prefer to use individual letters, each paragraph in #198 could be used as the text for a separate letter.

#198   (Form Letter)

December 3, 19___

Ms. Jane Doe
1473 Suburban St.
Anytown, Nev. 00000

Dear Customer:

Thank you for writing. Please see the paragraphs checked below for our reply.

☐1. The order blanks you requested are enclosed.

☐2. We are sorry, but we cannot comply with your request. All delayed orders for _____ have been shipped or refunds have been made. If you receive this merchandise and cannot use it, please fill out the enclosed form and return it to us with the merchandise by Parcel Post.

☐3. All delayed orders for _____ have now been shipped or refunds have been made. If your order or refund does not arrive within 10 days, please notify us, enclosing all papers. Upon receiving this information we will proceed according to your instructions.

☐4. Our records indicate that your order for _____
_____ has been shipped, but we have put a tracer on the lost shipment. If the merchandise does not reach you within 10 days, please notify us, returning all the papers we have sent you. We shall be happy to make whatever settlement you wish.

Yours very truly,

Customer Service

Enc.

Blaming the Computer

Rightly or wrongly, blaming the computer continues to be a popular dodge for explaining errors. Certainly the customer is helpless to argue with it, although he may eventually decide to take his business to a place where old-fashioned human hands get involved. The following brief letter is useful in many situations, with slight changes.

#199   (Letterhead)

March 3, 19____

Mr. James Jones
3453 Popular St.
Anytown, Wy. 00000

Dear Sir:

A computer error was responsible for the mix-up in your account (or order). We regret any inconvenience it may have caused you. The situation has now been rectified and our check for the amount due you is enclosed.

Sincerely,

Accounting Dept.

Here are variations of the same letter:

(a) A computer error was responsible for the mix-up in your order. We regret any inconvenience it may have caused you. The situation has now been rectified and the missing merchandise is on its way to you, together with a corrected invoice. Thank you for your patience and understanding.

(b) A computer error was responsible for the mix-up in your account. The situation has now been rectified, and your account is marked Paid in Full. We regret any inconvenience that may have been caused you.

(c) A computer mishap was responsible for the errors in the invoice sent you. The situation has now been rectified and a corrected invoice is enclosed. We apologize for any inconvenience that may have been caused you.

Letters Concerning Lost or Damaged Merchandise

#200   (Letterhead)

April 10, 19___

Mr. John Doe
1012 Any St.
Anytown, Tx. 00000

Dear Mr. Doe:

Repairs on the watch you sent us in November were completed promptly and the watch was mailed to you December 10, 19___. We can only assume that the watch was lost in transit. Since it was insured, we have reported the matter to the Post Office.

We should have a report within two weeks or so. If the watch is found it will be sent to you promptly. If the Post Office cannot locate the watch, a check for the declared value will be sent to you. We are sorry for the inconvenience and worry that has been caused you, but the situation was beyond our control. These things do happen in a very small percentage of cases.

Yours very truly,

Customer Relations Dept.

#201   (Letterhead)

October 12, 19___

Mr. John Doe
1904 Broad St.
Bigtown, Fla. 00000

Dear Sir:

We regret to say that we can find no record of our having received the merchanidse you sent us. We suggest that you contact the carrier (or the

Post Office), presenting your receipt. They should either locate the merchandise or reimburse you for its loss.

Yours very truly,

Complaint Dept.

#202   (Letterhead)

May 25, 19___

Mrs. Richard Roe
1419 Busy St.
Anytown, Colo. 00000

Dear Mrs. Roe:

We are very sorry to hear that the Ginger Jar you ordered, catalog #0578-T, was damaged in delivery. Please return the merchandise to us as soon as possible, and a replacement will be sent. For mailing to us, place the original carton containing the merchandise and all packing material inside a larger carton addressed to us, <u>JOHN DOE CO., 23 FRONT ST., ANYTOWN, IL. 00000, DEPT. 47.</u> On the outside of the package please attach an envelope enclosing a copy of your letter to us. This procedure is necessary for insurance purposes. We will send you a check for the return postage when the damaged merchandise is received.

Thank you for your cooperation. We hope that you have not been unduly inconvenienced. All John Doe Co. merchandise is packed with great care and is fully insured, but once in a great while something beyond our control does cause difficulty.

Yours very truly,

Jane Smith
Customer Service, Dept. 47

CHAPTER *11*

Advertising and Sales Letters
That Bring Results

In a more leisurely era, before TV, sales letters could depend to a certain extent on their entertainment value to attract the reader. Jokes and elegant literary introductions were often used in the hope of luring the prospective customer down a primrose path to the ultimate message. In their time these letters often worked satisfactorily. If they did not, who was counting?

Nowadays, unless they are very, very good, quick and sharp, such introductions merely act as a barrier between the reader and your message. One glance of his sophisticated eye, and the customer thinks he is being conned. He will not even read your cute story, much less get down to your message.

In a way, except for a few brilliant exceptions, the value of the old indirect approach was always doubtful. If the message was not compelling in itself, it is highly unlikely that an introductory joke was going to make it so.

Get Your Message Across Quickly

The basic problem of the modern letter-writer is to get his message across quickly, and to tie it in so adroitly with the prospective customer's interests that the customer will respond to the message.

How long should the letter be? The answer to that is that it should be just long enough to tell your story and to stimulate action by the reader. Every now and again a vogue for very long sales letters crops up — letters that are three, five even ten pages long. Based on my experience, and on common sense, most such letters are far less effective than the good one-page letter.

Your customers, like yourself, are deluged with reading material nowadays, all of it competing with television and other time-consuming things. A great many people will be appalled at the sight of a ten-page sales letter. If the letter dallies about getting to the point, the money was badly misspent for all that paper and labor. Nine out of ten times such a letter is headed unread for the waste basket.

There is rule number one — Be brief. Tell your customer as quickly and clearly and dramatically as you can what it is about your product or service that makes it absolutely essential to him.

List Your Selling Points, Plan the Letter

Before you begin your sales letter, sit down and list the selling points of your product — what makes it desirable, what makes it stand out above all others. If the main selling point is price, a saving, hang your letter on that. If it is durability, dramatize that. If it is better service, lighter weight, or more speed that interests the people who buy your product, then use these to do your selling in the letter directed to new prospects.

Remember as you write that flowery style and wit are not important. The straightforward presentation of your story will do the job better. The test of the merit of the letter is in the results. If the customer reads it and turns and writes you a check, or grabs his car keys and comes to your store, it is of far more value to you than having him praise your elegant literary style. You are not in a writing contest. You are in a selling contest.

Read the following letters and notice their simplicity, their directness. You can use them as models for your own sales letters.

Some Models for Straightforward, Hard-hitting Letters

#203   (Letterhead)

August 4, 19____

Mr. Andrew Smith, Mgr.
Distributing Center
Big Food Wholesale Co.
9041 Outlying Rd.
Bigtown, N.J. 00000

Dear Mr. Smith:

If you are tired of excessive maintenance costs on delivery trucks eating into your company's profits, we believe we can show you how to cut those costs by at least 10% a year. Study after study by independent auditors—with hard figures you can check—all prove that this is so.

Atlas Scheduled Maintenance Stops Truck Breakdowns.

Atlas scheduled maintenance stops truck trouble before it stops your trucks—practically eliminates highway breakdowns, cuts lost man hours, preserves good customer relations. Even in a moderate-sized business the savings in dollars and cents are well worth while. The Atlas monthly charge is well below the actual and hidden costs of haphazard care. Atlas takes full responsibility for maintaining your fleet in top condition at all times. Think what that means in peace of mind as well as money.

I am enclosing a leaflet showing a picture of our giant diagnostic center and our thoroughly modern shop. You are invited to inspect these at any time.

I should greatly appreciate an opportunity to explain all the benefits of Atlas' money-saving service to you. Perhaps I can accompany you on a tour of the diagnostic center and shop. Please telephone me at 000-3497, and we can set a date for any time you say.

Yours very truly,

Richard Roe
Customer Contact Representative

Enc.

An Unusual Appeal from a Furniture Company

Sometimes a letter can be sent to a neglected market and it will bring a nice increase in business. Someone at an office furniture company realized one day that doctors' and dentists' waiting rooms contain a lot of furniture. The idea inspired the following appeal. Such a letter should be sent to the physician's home, because anything not pertaining to drugs or technical equipment would probably be screened out by the doctor's office personnel.

#204   (Letterhead)

January 12, 19____

Dr. L.G. Kent
3914 Elegant St.
Suburbanville, R.I. 00000

Dear Dr. Kent:

I am sure you are up-to-date in everything else — but what about your waiting room? How long is it since you gave the waiting room a good examination, or even observed it as a patient would? What condition are the chairs in? How is the lighting? Is the carpet past its prime? And the color scheme — pretty drab, eh?

Now is an excellent time to have that waiting room redone, make it reflect your capable, modern approach. After you have made your selections, perhaps with the help of our coordinated decorator groupings, Quality Office Furniture can take care of the change without interrupting your schedule.

A Week-End Is All It Takes Us to Modernize
the Setup As You Wish

Come to our showroom at 2012 Business St. any evening before 10 (excepting Sunday) or come on the weekend. Our experts will help you select from coordinated, handsome furnishings in several price ranges. If your time is limited, just dial 000-2398, and our representative will call on you at your convenience, bringing color photographs and samples of carpets and materials.

Either way, your choice can be quickly made. And then we set to work. Any weekend you choose, our men will whisk out the old furniture and accessories and set up the new things—even lay a new carpet, put up new drapes, if they are included. (The old furnishings will be stored for you at a small charge, or delivered to any place you direct.)

How about it, Doctor? Isn't it about time your waiting room got a new outlook? Telephone 000-2398 now, and let the Quality man show you what beautiful furnishings are available.

Sincerely,

Professional Decor Div.

In a letter like #204 addressed to doctors and other professionals there is a temptation to fall into puns and cuteness. Don't do it. Every professional person has already heard all the alleged witticisms connected with his field, and they will only detract from the force and sincerity of your message.

The envelope for the above letter deserves some thought. You may wish to leave off your firm name and use only the street address. You might imprint some message on the envelope to excite interest, such as a line: About Your Waiting Room. . . .

#205   (Letterhead)

October 3, 19___

Mr. Richard Roe
2124 Residential St.
Suburbanville, Or. 00000

Dear Customer:

It is here at last — the Hearing Aid that NORMALIZES impaired hearing, rather than amplifying the full range of sound as others do. This new instrument is fantastically small. It is about the size of a shirt stud! So small it can be implanted in the ear, if you and your physician decide on this. (Of course it need not be implanted.)

Each Microminiature Hearing Aid is Custom-Modulated
at the Factory to Suit Your Precise Hearing Needs.

John Doe Co.'s experts will test you to find the exact areas of hearing loss you may have. A chart that is a detailed reading of your needs, and only yours, will be sent to the factory. There trained technicians will modify the tiny electronic components off the shelf to fit your chart precisely.

Then and there, your own <u>prescription hearing aid</u> will be assembled. It will be sent off to us in a matter of days, ready for you to pick up.

Just trying out one of these Microminiature Aids that is merely <u>close</u> to your needs (we have a wide assortment for pre-testing) will be a revelation to you—yet it will be only an approximation of the custom modulated model that will be made to order for you. The great difference with the Microminiature Aid is that it takes into account the fact that every person's hearing loss pattern is different.

If you have lost only the high notes, that is what your Microminiature will restore. Why should you have the low sounds amplified in addition, to boom out from your hearing aid? If you have lost some high notes and some intermediate tones, these, and these only, will be restored to you.

<u>Whatever Your Precise Need, You Will Be</u>
<u>Given Normal-Seeming Hearing Again</u>!

If you think this all sounds unbelievable, you are invited to come to John Doe Co. and try out the test instruments. Take all the time you wish. There is no obligation. We keep 60 variously tuned Microminiature Aids in a case about the size of a cigarette package! They look rather like pearls, and they are far more precious—yet even the customized models are surprisingly low-priced.

Telephone now for an appointment to see and try the amazing Microminiatures. We'll grant you a full hour, if you wish.

Telephone <u>000-2949</u>. Do it now!

Yours very truly,

John Doe, President

THE NEW MICROMINIATURE HEARING AID IS EXCLUSIVE
WITH JOHN DOE & CO. IN YOUR CITY.

This letter selling an imaginary hearing aid is an example of the amount of information, as well as selling power, that can be packed into a one-page letter. Note how underlining is used to break up the mass of type and to highlight the selling points.

In telling such a sensational story the temptation might be to use too much underlining. Restrain this impulse, because if too much material is underlined, then nothing stands out. Use underlining like a rare spice.

If you have a new product to sell, or one that needs explaining, study the hearing aid letter carefully. It seems spontaneous, yet it has been carefully planned. The first paragraph tells the whole story briefly, then the two underlined lines retell the major story, very briefly. Following this, several paragraphs elaborate on the story, applying the custom-modulated feature to the customer himself, as an individual.

After this, the story is summarized again in two emphasized lines but in different words.

The next paragraph lures the customer to action with an intriguing offer. The two brief paragraphs at the end practically put the telephone in his hand.

Repetition is extremely valuable in building up excitement and in making complicated features clear. To plan such a letter, imagine yourself telling the wonderful news of a new product to a friend. You would do it in exactly this way. You would blurt out the whole story first, then you would explain and explain some more.

For the first draft of your letter, write out the story just as you would tell it. This gives you a start, something to work with. Before you have finished you will make additions, transpose portions, change some wording here and there . . . . but the spontaneity and force of your enthusiastic first draft should remain in the finished product. Close the letter with a clincher that says, "telephone 000-0000 now" or "mail the enclosed card now."

One more point. Ordinarily the actual price of the item should be mentioned, perhaps even made to stand out. This is important, because if you do not mention the price, the reader will surely assume that it is too high.

The case of the miraculous hearing aid is a little different. Here the writer is actually selling the idea of the reader's coming into the store to try out this wonder, whether or not he can afford it. The price is undoubtedly high, and in a way it is a good idea to prepare the customer for this, as applied to this particular item. If you are acquainted with any deaf persons, you know they would pay any price to secure the modulated, normal hearing this imaginary aid promises. (Perhaps by the time this is printed they will have it.)

#206   (Letterhead)

                                                    March 1, 19___

Advance News for You! (Written in smart script across the top of letter.)

Mrs. J.R. Smith
3092 Posh St.
Suburbantown, N.Y. 00000

Dear Preferred Customer:

Mark these dates on your calendar: <u>March 8th</u>, <u>9th</u> and <u>10th</u>. These are advance shopping days for our preferred customers, so that you can have first choice of the tremendous values we have assembled for

<u>John Doe Co.'s Pre-Easter Sale!</u>

You can shop in advance of the crowds, pick and choose at your leisure. No news of this tremendous money-saving event will appear in the newspapers until the evening of the 10th.

Signs throughout each store will designate the sale specials—and what specials they are! Brand new spring merchandise has been marked down as much as 25% for the Pre-Easter Sale. You will save many dollars on your Easter outfit, and on other springtime needs as well. Here are a few highlights from among hundreds of sale features:

<u>Catalina Double-Knit</u> <u>Sportswear!</u>	<u>Laird, Schober Shoes,</u> <u>a Special Selection!</u>
<u>Koret Permanent-Press</u> <u>Jackets, Pants, and</u> <u>Skirts!</u>	<u>Finer Fur-Trimmed Coats</u> <u>25% Under Price!</u>
<u>Butte Knits!</u>	<u>Brand New Millinery</u> <u>Arrivals!</u>
<u>Boys' and Girls' Wear!</u>	<u>Many Men's Wear Specials!</u>

Remember the dates—Tuesday, Wednesday, and Thursday—March 8th, 9th and 10th. Come prepared to save on all the springtime needs of the whole family! All sale merchandise available at all three John Doe Stores.

                                        Yours very truly,

                                        John Doe, President

Advertising letters have some of the appeal of personal letters, but you can take quite a few liberties with them without sacrificing that appeal. In the above letter, that handwritten line across the top lends "color," gets attention, and helps to insure that the message will be read. Once again, as in many good advertising letters, discreet use of underlining and tabulation adds to the interesting appearance of the letter. It also directs the eye to important points. A solid page of typewriting can be pretty dull looking without the use of such devices.

For further pointers on enhancing the appearance and readability of letters, see Chapter 15.

Letters Selling an Additional Service or Product

If for some time you have been selling a customer one thing, although you have several to offer, take advantage of this when writing your advertising letter. Your selling job is already half done, because you are known and your letter will surely be read and considered.

Here is a letter that makes good use of such a situation:

#207   (Letterhead)

                                                  August 12, 19___

Mrs. Rita Roe
Outstanding Hotel
1742 Downtown St.
Big City, Neb. 00000

Dear Mrs. Roe:

We have been pleased to serve you and Outstanding Hotel for some years with our famous institutional laundry service. As you know, our laundry work is outstanding in quality, prompt delivery, and economical pricing. This being so, we are hoping now that Superior Laundry may also serve you and Outstanding Hotel with <u>Dry Cleaning Service</u>. Yes, we have recently opened a thoroughly modern dry cleaning plant, especially designed to serve the needs of hotels and institutions. Moreover, we are making a special offer to our regular laundry customers for the entire month of September.

<u>Special 10% Discount During September</u>
<u>on 50 Pounds or More of Dry Cleaning!</u>

Your regular Superior Laundry man will collect your draperies, bed-spreads, and anything else dry cleanable, on any day you say. <u>He will bring</u> <u>them back three days later,</u> radiantly clean and beautiful—all at 10% discount from our regular low prices. Give us a call now and tell us when to have your Superior Man pick up your dry cleaning. We know you will be delighted with the quality of our superb cleaning service.

Telephone 000-9487 for prompt pickup. Save 10% on all fall cleaning!

Yours for clean thinking,

John Doe, Manager

Getting Outside Your Subject to Achieve Drama

Some advertising letters use a striking situation to rivet the reader's attention, before going on to the details of the thing being sold. To write such letters, imagine yourself as the customer. Think of what he or she does or thinks that makes your product necessary. Visualize a situation he might be in that would make your product indispensable. Write down your thoughts, then phrase your lead-in concisely and dramatically.

In the first letter below this approach is used to tell a story which is important, but which could be dull if just factually told.

#208   (Letterhead)

October 5, 19___

Mrs. Robert Hughes
2114 Pleasant Lane
Suburbanville, N.J. 00000

Dear Mrs. Hughes:

<u>More Red Ribbon and Less Red Tape!</u> That's what Blank Bros. Depart-ment Store is promising you for this Christmas season, because we believe Christmas shopping should be merrier.

We've hired extra salespeople, extra wrappers!
We've streamlined and speeded up our service
to cut down on waiting!

Blank Bros. is going all out to give you some real, old-fashioned service. We think our customers will appreciate it in these days of self-service and customer-neglect. Our prices? We think you will find them quite reasonable—within a few pennies of the so-called discount prices.

And then there are our gift boxes that add so much to the quality look of your gifts. This year they will be snowy white, with a touch of gold, and lavishly tied with red ribbon! All except the tiniest ones will have a spray of make-believe holly added. (More elaborate custom wraps also available.)

Plan now to do all your Christmas shopping at Blank's, in a smiling atmosphere of service. Our gorgeous Christmas decorations are up, and we are all set to serve you. Use your Blank's charge card or your bank card.

To Defer All Payments Till February On Your Blank's Charge
Account, Use the Red Ribbon Stickers that are Enclosed

Just hand the salesperson one of your Red Ribbon Stickers when you give her your Blank's Charge Card. She will affix the stickers to your salescheck, and you will not be billed or charged interest until February 1 of next year.

Make your Christmas list tonight, and come to Blank Bros. tomorrow. You will see what we mean by "More Red Ribbon and Less Red Tape."

Yours for Merrier Christmas Shopping,

John Doe Blank, President

The above letter is an example of what is called "institutional" advertising. The quality and personality of the store are being sold. A high-pressure letter advertising a sale or a price cut would not need the catchy lead-in theme. It would only detract from the main story in such a case.

A High-Pressure Direct-Selling Letter

The next letter uses an incident from someone's life to lure the reader into the selling message. (The letter is aimed at selling another very useful book by the author of this one!)

#209 (Letterhead)

March 3, 19____

Mr. Henry Van Arsdale
2223 Broad St.
Bigtown, Pa. 00000

Dear Reader:

. . . ."And there I was, struck dumb at this crucial point, while he talked on and on. I knew he was wrong, but I could not regain control of the discussion. I could not think of a thing to say"

Have you ever been involved in this sort of business nightmare, when a sudden turn of events wrecks all your plans, makes you feel like an incompetent?

It need never happen again.

Experts in human relations have at their fingertips certain key words and phrases to use in any such situation, special techniques that brush aside the opposition and put the expert back in the driver's seat instantly. What are these key words and phrases, these special techniques? You can find them all, spotlighted and fully explained, in a fascinating book available from Parker Publishing Co., Inc. The book is:

HOW TO PUT YOURSELF ACROSS WITH KEY WORDS AND PHRASES

by Martha W. Cresci

Here's a book that puts the words in your mouth so you'll come out ahead in any conversation, argument or discussion. Listening to the experts, analyzing their methods during a lifetime of experience in the business world, the author has written for you a compendium of the key words and phrases and shows you how to use them in any crucial situation that may come up—shows you how to use them and win! Also revealed are the magic words that can bring raises, promotions and prestige for you.

No executive, no one who hopes to become a top executive, can afford to be without this amazing book. Consider these chapter headings, taken at random from the table of contents—consider what such information may mean to you:

- How to Use Skillful Flattery to Ease Difficult Situations.
- How to Use the Banal to Solve Problem Situations.
- How to Win—or Lose—an Argument Advantageously.
- How to Tell the Boss He Misunderstood.

- How to Polish Your Image—Quickly.
- Creating Loyalty in Your Staff.
- Making the Formal Presentation Your Big Opportunity.
- Social Situations with the Boss—How to Make Them Pay Off.

All this, and much more, is covered. The actual words and phrases the expert manipulators use are put down in black and white, and their use is dramatically explained so that you will have them at the tip of your tongue, to serve <u>you</u>. You need never be at a loss for words—success-building words—in any difficult situation. Send for the book today.

Fill in the enclosed order card now and send it with your check in the return envelope. Take command of your career from this moment on.

Yours for success,

John Doe
Parker Publishing Co., Inc.

The general form of the book letter can be used to sell any merchandise—a cookbook . . . beauty aids . . . cleaning products. . . . Just about anything. Notice how it applies the product to the reader's own life, how the explanations are repeated over and over again with further development. Note also that mostly short words are used, and the tempo is exciting. At the end the reader is exhorted to act immediately, with short explicit instructions.

Such letters have to be high pressure, they have to incite immediate action, because they are competing with a thousand activities and events in a busy person's day. If the reader is not persuaded to act immediately, he may very well forget, or even lose the letter.

The Same Type of Letter Used to Sell Ceramic Ware

Study the next letter and compare it with the foregoing one. You will see that it is strikingly similar in structure and technique. Instead of the dramatic incident at the beginning of the book letter, we use a wish-fulfilling phrase.

#210   (Letterhead)

August 2, 19___

Mrs. Harrison Jones
2019 Residential St.
Suburbanville, Io. 00000

Never Wash Pans Again! (Handwritten on a slant in a bold, script.)

Dear Mrs. Jones:

We said it and we mean it: NEVER WASH PANS AGAIN!

You can now do all your cooking in beautiful Ceramic Ware — cook and serve food in the same lovely dishes! Boil, fry, roast, bake — do it all in Ceramic Ware. Freeze food in the same dishes, if you wish. These beautiful utensils, made of the same amazing ceramic used in missile cones, can go from freezer to stove to table. You then slip them into the dishwasher or the sink with the other dishes. Never slave at scouring pans again!

<u>Come See Ceramic Cookware Demonstrated</u>
in Big Store's Housewares Department

Wednesday, Thursday, Friday
<u>August 8th, 9th and 10th</u>

Handle these Ceramic cook-and-serve pieces. Test and try them yourself. See how practically and beautifully they have been designed. Note how easily the clever lifting handle clicks on and off. Then stock up. As you can see by the enclosed brochure, prices are surprisingly reasonable.

Yours very truly,

Housewares Buyer

P.S. You may order by mail or telephone if you can't come in for the demonstration. Call 000-9378 till 9 P.M.

Letters like this, plus newspaper advertising, based on my phrase "Never Wash Pans Again" set new sales records for Corning Ware in our city when this famous ceramic cookware was first introduced. Such phrases are easy to think up. Just put yourself in the customer's place.

I used a similar slogan to set records for the sale of a leading line of permanent-press clothes when permanent-press was new. That line was "Never Iron Clothes Again!" It was followed up, of course, by all the positive selling points that pertained to the permanent-press fashions that were being promoted. Other such lines you may find useful as models are: "Don't Walk Miles to Do Your Shopping"; "You Needn't Spend a Fortune for Top Fashion"; "Throw Out Those Pens that Don't Work"; "You, Too, Can Be an Expert Handyman".

Some Pointers on Selling Merchandise by Mail

Unless the merchandise being offered is very familiar, or like the hearing aid (#205) can be vividly described, letters are not the best advertising medium. A small mail order company, for instance, should lean toward mailing pieces that can accompany explicit description with very realistic illustrations. On the other hand, there are some types of merchandise that can be handled very well by letters. Here are some examples:

#211   (Letterhead)

February 2, 19____

Mrs. John La Chance
2417 Residential Lane
San Anselmo, Ca. 00000

Dear Madam:

With Easter less than nine weeks away, you are probably already planning the Easter outfits for yourself and the children. You will be delighted to know that you can save tremendously on better quality fabrics right now.

Metropolitan Fabric Co.'s Pre-Easter
SALE OF NEW SPRING FABRICS BEGINS FEBRUARY 6th!
Savings of 1/4 to 1/3!

36000 yards of the most exciting fabric fashions you will see this spring are included. Hundreds of new bolts have just been unpacked. New spring colors, including crayon blue and the other exciting bright tones, plus pastels and white. Tiny flower prints, big splashy prints, checks, stripes, plaids . . . they are all here. All fabrics are no-iron, of course. Scoop them up and save on everything you sew for spring, whether it's suits, dresses, or children's outfits. Make your list tonight and be here early. Here are a few of the scores of specials:

Doubleknit Polyester, solids, checks. plaids, 1/4 Off–$0.00 yd.

Doubleknit Polyesters in multi-color small prints, 1/4 Off–$0.00 yd.

Qiana Nylon Prints, luxuriously soft pastels, 1/4 Off–$0.00 yd.

Polyester Crepes, brilliant splashy prints, now 1/3 Off–$0.00 yd.

Handsome, Sturdy Denims, blue, red, green, yellow, 1/3 Off–$0.00 yd.

Nylon-Blend Voiles in new "shadow" prints, 1/4 Off, Now–$0.00 yd.

Polyester-Blend Piques, white and solid shades, 1/3 Off–$0.00 yd.

I look forward to serving you. The sale is for 10 days only–beginning Friday, February 6th. Be early!

Sincerely,

Anna Mae Smith, Mgr.

A footnote on the above letter: it is axiomatic in advertising circles that "new" is the one word that will never wear out. In the world of fashion, especially, it is always powerful.

The next letter is fine for its purpose, because it will assuredly be sent to a selected list of people in luxury homes, and because the merchandise is familiar to them. Another factor involved is that the merchandise cannot be done justice by any illustration. A letter similarly conceived could sell Limoges china, expensive furs, or top-name automobiles. Actually, the letter will sell the customer the idea of coming in to be sold. Such letters should be printed beautifully on fine quality stationery.

#212   (Letterhead)

September 9, 19____

Mrs. J. Rutherford Spencer
15 Opulent Blvd.
Suburbantown, N.Y. 00000

Dear Madam:

Abkarian Bros. Co. is proud to announce the showing of one hundred-nine superb Oriental Rugs at our Madison Avenue showroom, beginning Monday, September 10th.

These richly beautiful floorcoverings were individually selected by Mr. William Abkarian himself in an extended trip through Iran, Iraq, Saudi Arabia, and Afghanistan. Each one is a prize, to be treasured by a discriminating homeowner. All but three are in very good to excellent condition. (The three that are in fair to good condition are very old Bokharas, chosen for the collectors among our customers.)

Each rug, as you know, is different, and each is a masterpiece of the ancient art, hand-tied throughout. A surprising number of larger rugs are included. Mr. William Abkarian will be happy to serve you personally by appointment, if you wish, giving the history of each magnificent selection.

Priced according to size and quality, the following groups are included:

Baluchistans .	$000 to $0000	Bokharas . . .	$0000 to $00000
Uskudars . .	$0000 to $0000	Hamams . . .	$000 to $0000
Kashans . . .	$000 to $0000	Kermanshas .	$000 to $0000
Hamadans . .	$000 to $0000	Isfahans	$000 to $000
Kermans . .	$0000 to $0000	Sarouks . . .	$0000 to $0000

You may drop in at our showroom at your convenience, or you may telephone for an appointment with Mr. William Abkarian for a personal showing, whichever you prefer. Those who act promptly will be assured of the widest selection, of course. Our telephone number is 000-0000. Hours are 10 to 5:30, Monday through Friday. We look forward to the pleasure of serving you.

Sincerely,

Abkarian Bros. Co.

In any listing of items, as in the above letter, when all type is the same size, arrange the order carefully. Put the most desirable item at the bottom of the list, the second most desirable at the beginning. Sandwich the less desirable items in between. Studies have shown that most people remember longest the last item on the list, and remember next longest the first item on the list.

A Letter Selling Cheap Mail Order Items
Without Illustrations

In contrast to the dignity and subtle flattery of the Oriental Rug letter, note the pressure and the emphasis on price in the next letter. Note that all the items are either very familiar to everyone or things that can be easily described, thus making illustrations unnecessary. Another important point about the mail order letter is that it should give some plausible reason that explains the low prices—preferably a one-time happening.

#213   (Letterhead)

March 23, 19____

Mr. George Jackson
1314 Any St.
Any Town, Del. 00000

Dear Sir:

John Doe Bargain Co. has just received an assortment of distress merchandise, negotiated by our traveling representative, which presents some spectacular buys. Every item offered is brand new, perfect quality merchandise that sells everywhere at double these prices—but QUANTITIES ARE STRICTLY LIMITED.

Check This List and Order Now. When These Are Gone
There Will Be No More at Such Prices

540 Bean Bag Ashtrays—00¢ ea.
Polished brass-finished ashtray fastened to soft vinyl bean bag in green or red.

205 Desk Pen Sets—$0.00 ea.
Gorgeous quality, great for gifts, prizes. Two desk pens and calendar on simulated onyx base. Were $10.95.

Men's Orlon Socks—6 pairs $0
Heavy, rich quality regularly twice this price and more. Olive or yellow, one color to bundle. Sizes 10-13. State size and color. Shrink-proof.

5-Year Diaries Below ½-Price—00¢

Current year Diaries, 6" x 8." Simulated leather cover, gold-embossed. No color choice at this price. Worth $0.00

Ladies' Nylon Pantyhose—00¢

Minimum order 6 pairs at this fantastic price. One size fits all reg. sizes. Beige or taupe, state choice.

Playing Cards—2 Decks $0

Plastic finish, bridge size. Gorgeous backs. Sold in pairs. Order for clubs, prizes, your own use, and save.

Tear Off This ORDER BLANK and Mail It Now
in Enclosed PREPAID ENVELOPE

To: John Doe Bargain Co.
     2112 Busy St.
     Outlying Town, N.J. 00000

Date _____

Name _____

Address _____

City _____ State _____

Zip Code (Must be given.) _____

Please find enclosed:

My Name Bank Card #_____

My personal check, amount
     $_____

Money Order, amount $_____

     (Do not send cash or stamps.)

Satisfaction Guaranteed
Or Your Money Back

Quantity

_____ Ashtrays @ 00¢. Color _____
_____, Total price $_____

_____ Orlon Socks, _____ bundles of 6 pr. Color _____. Size
_____ Total $_____

_____ Pairs Pantyhose, 6 pr. $0.
Minimum order 6 pr. Color _____
Total $_____

_____ $0.00 Pen Sets, Total $_____

_____ Diaries @ 00¢, Total $_____

_____ Decks Cards, 2 for $0,
Total $_____

This mail order letter, if single-spaced will fit on one page. If yours does not quite make it, ask the printer to reduce it ever so slightly. Take his advice as to the feasibility of reducing it. Do not sacrifice legibility and good arrangement. Cut your copy or run to two pages if necessary.

Other Factors Involved in the Success of Advertising Letters

Advertising letters are patently one of the most economical and productive forms of advertising. They have an important place in the balanced promotional programs of many giant corporations. For some businesses they are actually the most suitable form of advertising. Lastly, the low cost of advertising letters may make them the only practical form of advertising to be considered by many small businesses that are reaching out for more customers. In all cases, the most resultful use of letters takes considerable planning.

To Whom Shall We Send the Letter? Selecting a List

If yours is a business with a roster of charge customers, this list will usually produce the most sales in ratio to the number of letters sent. On the other hand, if you are striving to attract new customers you may wish to buy or rent a list of selected new prospects. There are firms in every city that specialize in compiling mailing lists, and the variety obtainable is astounding. Costs are moderate.

A variety store owner may decide to send his letter indiscriminately to all the heads of households within a twenty-block radius of his store. He can order such a list, or, if he wishes, have the list company address and mail his letters to a selected area. Other businesses may wish to send a letter to lawyers only, to doctors only, or to a general list of persons with incomes over $50,000 per year. All these are obtainable at a moment's notice, as are lists of farmers, car owners, and countless other special groups. In some cases the Yellow Pages of your telephone directory will prove an excellent source of names.

How Many Letters Shall We Send? Figuring Costs

Deciding how many letters you will mail depends on several factors, not the least of which is the money involved. If third class postage is 5¢ each, 10,000 letters will cost $500 for postage alone.

Add to that the cost of paper, envelopes, printing, addressing, stuffing and sorting. If you use your own letterhead stationery, the paper cost will probably be higher than if certain papers are supplied by the printer.

If you are on an absolutely minimum budget, you may want to investigate the so-called instant printing. For this you have your letter cleanly typed on your letterhead, or any chosen paper, sign it in black ink, and the whole thing is reproduced on a less expensive paper at surprisingly low cost.

A concomitant factor in your decision as to how many letters to print, is the matter of how much you expect to get out of them. Balance this against the cost of the letters. The length of your mailing list will of course be involved in the decision also.

What Is a Good Return on a Letter?

A response from 3% to 5% of the people who receive your letter is considered good when the letter is sent to a generalized list. Very appealing letters sent to highly-selective lists may occasionally produce as high as 10% return, or even 20% in rare cases. A great deal depends on the demand for the thing being offered, as well as the appeal of the letter. Return, self-addressed envelopes or cards increase returns, when appropriate, especially if they are postpaid. Gimmicks such as coupons, tickets, etc. are helpful in some cases. Imprinting the envelope with a powerful message may help to insure that the envelope will be opened, but this can be overdone.

A letter going to the charge customers of a well-known business will almost always be opened if it just bears the return address. Other envelopes may get help from such imprinted phrases as the following:

> Important Information About Your Car.
> A Notice Concerning Your Subscription.
> News of a Once-a-Year Money-Saving Event!
> Your 20% Discount Card Is Enclosed.
> About Your Waiting Room. . . .
> Not All Children Are Bad Mannered. . . .

The last two of these are called "teasers." They are mysterious and tantalizing, but they do apply to the message inside the envelope. If you think a teaser will help to get your letter read, by all means use it; but make it a good one.

Methods to Insure Getting Replies

A letter going by itself, without enclosures, must depend on the message it carries, plus its form, to elicit replies. Every letter must do three things:

1. Excite interest immediately.
2. Convince the reader he must have the product or service.
3. Make him act. It must make him either telephone, write, fill in and mail a card or coupon, or come to your place of business.

Steps one and two lead up to step three, but they do not make step three inevitable. You have to force that action by, in effect, commanding it. Finish off every letter with a command, more or less polite, as: Telephone 000-0000 now. Order now—call 000-0000. Telephone now for an appointment—call 000-0000. Come in tomorrow, as supplies are limited. Mail the coupon now!

Gimmicks and Enclosures Used to Increase Response

A good letter by itself can often do a very good job; but if you can afford it you may wish to give it some help. If your letter is soliciting mail orders for merchandise, a return envelope enclosed may increase orders tenfold or more. This is especially true if the return pre-addressed envelope is postage-paid. Consider this fact carefully in planning the budget for your letter. Consult with the post office to see if you can arrange to pay postage only on the envelopes mailed back to you.

A return postcard instead of the envelope may serve the same purpose. In sales of merchandise the order-coupon could be placed on the back of the postcard. In some cases you may wish to enclose the envelope plus an order blank. When this is done, response may be boosted by printing the order blank on colored paper. The addition of color, for some reason, increases the number of replies. Perhaps it makes the package more interesting, or perhaps it is easier to keep track of among the many white papers on the desk. Pink has been found to be the most activating color; also for unknown reasons.

In letters addressed to women, concerning feminine subjects, it is a good idea to use social stationery rather than your letterhead. The stationery itself could be a pale pink. Of course, in a series of letters sent to the same list, the color should be varied to give variety, and to make it clear that later letters are not duplicates of the first.

Premiums and Gifts

Offering a premium or gift to a limited number of persons who respond to your offer is one gimmick used to increase response. Banks have used this successfully at times to boost the number of people coming in to open new accounts. You might use it to increase attendance at the opening of a new store.

Occasionally some sort of informative booklet is offered in a campaign to get a list of prospects for a brokerage house, a landselling outfit, or even an insurance company. The respondents receive their informative booklets, but they also become "leads" for the salesmen to follow up.

What Not to Do in Writing Sales Letters

One thing you should never do in composing your letter is to ask a question of the customer. Never say, "Don't you think so?" "Doesn't that sound great?" "Did you ever hear of an offer like this?"

If you ask a question you give the customer a chance to reply negatively ... at least in his thinking. You also interrupt the pattern of your letter, the drive toward the response you seek. Rather than question him, you want to tell him, explain to him, convince him, get him excited, and make him act.

An Example of a Bad Practice

Occasionally one sees a very bad practice become quite a vogue with advertisers. Heaven knows why this is so. Apparently one company does a thing and some thoughtless person in another company says, "Hey, that's different! We'll do it too!"

For a time, nearly every merchandise-selling letter I received in the mail infuriated me with a final sales-killing paragraph. You may remember it from among the letters you consigned to the waste basket.

After doing a creditable selling job, and perhaps enclosing expensive full-color brochures, the letter-writer killed off practically all hope of positive response by saying: *If for any reason you decide not to take advantage of this wonderful offer, I wish you would tell me why. I want to know this, because I am at a loss to understand why anyone would turn down this opportunity. Won't you please give me your reason on the enclosed card, and mail it back to me?*

What idiocy! The last thing you ever want to do, when you are trying to sell by letter, is to introduce the thought that your customer may not buy. To finish off your positive letter with this invitation to negative thinking is preposterous. Moreover, I, as a customer, found it insulting that the letter writer should question my judgment about what I wanted to buy.

Never succumb to fads like this. When in doubt, stick to the tried and true. You cannot go wrong with a straightforward, well composed letter. The news in the letter is enough to make it "different."

Writing Invitations That Bring Them In

Whatever the form, the most important thing about invitations is that they give all the facts. Check and re-check your copy to make sure you have covered all points—

Date.
Hour.
Place—with instructions for getting there, if necessary.
Refreshments?
Confirmation necessary?
Charge?
Formal or informal?
Telephone Number.

Probably the most important point of all is making it clear at a glance that your mailing piece *is* an invitation. Highlight the word or its equivalent.

It is amazing how many writers do not realize that not everyone examines every word of their deathless prose. Not comprehending this, many party-givers cut down response to events because the invitation is not immediately recognizable as such. An example is a beautifully printed card I received from a small art gallery.

On one side of the card was a fine reproduction of a charming painting, with the name of the painter and the name of the picture in small type underneath. Below the illustration was an ocean of white space, then, at the bottom, the name of the art gallery in large, elegant type. The biggest word on the other side of the card was "POTPOURRI," certainly a who-cares word for the art collector. If, in spite of this, the recipient happened to peer at the card, he would note in the small type that the card was an invitation to an important exhibition, scheduled for a certain date and hour, with refreshments.

Response to this tasteful mailing piece would almost surely have been doubled if the words "An Invitation" had been placed in the white space under the picture. Again, the words "You Are Invited" should have headlined the reverse side, followed by details, perhaps in this manner:

#214

You Are Invited
To An Important Exhibition
of Outstanding Works by
Eight Distinguished Artists

February Twenty-Eighth
6 to 8 P.M.   Refreshments

On display will be paintings by James
Bowers, Edward Brown, Susan Clark. Anna
Goodrich, John Guchi, Benjamin Johnson,
John Kenneth Watkins, and Beverly Wyatt.

J U N O   G A L L E R I E S
1109 A Street, Seaside   294-0000

The nice little word *potpourri* was sacrificed in this reworked invitation, because it was a subjective word that added nothing to the pull of the invitation. Beware of letting "cute" words and ideas interfere with your main message in any card or letter that is attempting to sell something. These brainchildren are fine if they add to the appeal of the piece; otherwise, they should be tenderly abandoned.

Other Types of Invitations

Some events are so obviously invitational that the word *invitation* need not be spotlighted. Among these are fashion shows, showings of new lines in almost any type of industry. Nevertheless, it should be made clear that those to whom mailing pieces are sent are invited to attend at a certain time on a certain day, if this is the case.

#215   (Letterhead or special stationery)

February 20, 19___

Mrs. R.B. Jones
921 Elegant Avenue
Suburbantown, Ariz. 00000

Dear Mrs. Jones:

The Fashion Boutique announces with pleasure that Mr. Joseph of Joseph Originals will conduct a private showing of his new spring designs in our store on Monday, March 3rd. at 2 P.M., and you are invited.

The Fashion Show, with Joseph Originals' own models, will be held in the Georgian Room, Fourth Floor. Refreshments will be served. Seating is limited, so reservations are requested. Please telephone now to make sure you can be present at this exciting event. Tell us how many will be in your party. The number to call is 444-0000.

The stunning Joseph Originals fashions to be modeled will include dresses for all occasions, suits, pantsuits, and sportswear. They are a must-see!

Sincerely,

THE FASHION BOUTIQUE

P.S. Remember the time—Monday, March 3rd at 2 P.M.
    Telephone 444-0000. Ask for Marcia Nemo.

Because there is so much that must be included in the above letter, the date, time and telephone number are repeated and spotlighted in the postscript.

#216   (Letterhead)

Mr. Earnest B. Armstrong, President
Technical Manufactures
2012 Industrial Way
Outlying City, Ind. 00000

Re: New Improvements In Computer Art — A Demonstration.

Dear Mr. Armstrong:

Mark Tuesday, September 14th on your calendar as a red letter day. On this day, at 10 A.M., you are invited to SPEAK to our astounding new VOICE-CONTROL COMPUTER. Command it, like a legendary genie, and it will serve you! Bring with you the most complex material your engineers and programmers can devise, to make your command a genuine test of this amazing advancement in computer art. Bring an actual problem if you wish.

Demonstrations Will Be Held All Day
Tuesday and Wednesday, Sept. 14 and 15
From 10 A.M. to 5 P.M.

If the appointment we have tentatively arranged for you and your group is not the best time for you, please telephone Henry Mason at 925-0000 for the time you prefer. This astounding advance in computers, the VOICE-CONTROL by Computer Dynamics is a must-see, must-try for every executive of a forward-looking industry in these days of cost consciousness.

Very truly yours,

Will Wilson, President
COMPUTER DYNAMICS

P.S. Please have your secretary telephone Henry Mason at 925-0000 now to confirm your appointment, so that time will be reserved for your group.

In both the preceeding invitations the postscript is essential. It is the "hook," made necessary by the fact that the story to be told is so involved. The reader may forget he is expected to call. In the postscript of the second letter the secretary is brought into the picture, so that the appointment will be put on the calendar.

#217 (Letterhead)

October 9, 19___

Mr. J. Eugene Powell, President
Belle Knitting Machines Co.
5142 Far Street
Bigtown, New Jersey 00000

Dear Mr. Powell:

For some time now B. & J. Co. has been producing three small parts, precision parts, that go into your justly famous knitting machines. (In a sense we are a part of you!) And yet we have never met you.

We should like to do something about that, if you agree.

Will you visit us?

I personally should like to show you through our great modern plant with its amazing automated machinery. I should like to introduce you to our people. I should like to treat you to lunch and dinner, and show you some of our southern hospitality in this pretty little city.

You are invited to drop in at the B. & J. plant any time you are near here—just ask the receptionist to buzz me. Better yet, if you will put down a date on the enclosed card, setting a specific time for your visit, and mail the card back to me, we will really roll out the red carpet. Please mail the card now, while you have it in mind.

Yours very truly,

Allan F. Burns, President

Enclosure

The card to accompany a letter such as the one to Mr. Powell should be pre-addressed and stamped. The wording would be something like the following:

Mr. Allan F. Burns, President
B. & J. Co., Blankville, S.C. 00000

I accept your invitation: How About (Month and Date) _____?
I plan to arrive (Time) _____ at the airport in Columbia.
Please meet me. OR I will drive down _____ , arriving (Time) _____ .
(Please indicate number in party.) I will be alone _____ .
OR I will be accompanied by (How many persons?) _____ .

PLEASE CONFIRM OUR APPOINTMENT.

Signature _____
Belle Knitting Machines Co.

CHAPTER 12

Announcements Fitted to
Their Purpose—Greetings

Some announcements must be just that and nothing more, because of ironclad rules governing the practices of certain professions. Luckily for most businesses, no such strictures apply, and announcements can be as varied as the imagination allows. You can often make your announcement do a terrific selling job, and you probably should. When you are spending money for a mailing, give the mailing piece plenty of thought and plan for maximum return on the dollar.

Examples of announcements included in this chapter run from the strictly formal to the colorful. Study them, and choose the type that will do your business the most good.

The first three announcements are the formal variety. They are usually printed or engraved in black ink on a white or cream card, such as those used for invitations to a wedding reception. Matching envelopes are used. Occasionally such an announcement may be printed or engraved on formal folded notepaper.

#218   (Formal card)

John Richmond Doe
Attorney at Law
Announces the Opening
of Law Offices
at 912 Center St., Anytown, N.J.
Wednesday, June 11, 19___

#219   (Formal card)

Dr. Richard Roe, Optometrist
Announces the Opening
of His New Office
in the Elegant Co. Dept. Store
Thursday, April 12—3rd Floor

Expert Fitting of Eyeglasses by Appointment. Telephone 000-0000

#220   (Formal card or odd size card, as preferred.)

Bigboard & Co., Stockbrokers
of 9212 Broad St. West
is Pleased to Announce
that Mr. John Tickertape
Has Joined Bigboard & Co.
as a Partner.

Mr. Tickertape will be in charge of all Mutual Fund Accounts

The last of these, since it is not so much restricted by tradition
and rules, might be written in the form of a dignified sales letter.

#220 (a)　　　　　　　　(Letterhead)

September 10, 19＿＿

Mr. Thornton Wheeler
1711 Pleasant St.
Suburbanville, Pa. 00000

Dear Mr. Wheeler:

Beginning September 12th, Bigboard & Co. is happy to announce that all
Mutual Fund Accounts at Bigboard will be handled in a separate department, under the direct supervision of a specialist in this type of investment. Mr. John Tickertape, who comes to us with highest credentials and a
reputation for outstanding success, is joining the firm as a full partner, in
charge of the important new Mutual Fund Dept.

If you have not yet met Mr. Tickertape, he will be pleased to have you
drop in for a discussion of your portfolio — or you may telephone ahead, if
you wish. The extension is 2412, at our regular number, 000-0000.

With very best regards,

J.L. Bigboard, President

Some More Colorful, More Inclusive Announcements

Businesses and professions that are not restricted by ironclad
rules can make announcement letters far more interesting and
arresting. If you have an announcement to make, use that announcement as a lead-in to a selling message. Some examples:

#221　　　　　　　　(Letterhead)

October 14, 19＿＿

Mrs. Harry Jones
1967 Residential Rd.
Suburbantown, N.C. 00000

Dear Neighbor:

When you are three years old, six, (or sixteen), happiness is being turned
loose in a LAUGHING GIANT TOY STORE right in your own neighbor-

hood. Now you can make that happiness come true for the youngsters you love, because:

<u>A New LAUGHING GIANT TOY STORE</u>
<u>is Being Opened Thursday, October 16th,</u>
<u>in Your Own Suburbantown Shopping Center!</u>

Bring the children! You need not worry about them, as we have two "Kiddie Watchers" constantly on duty to see that the children have fun, yet don't go too far in "examining" the merchandise. Bring your Christmas list, with you, by all means, for some early Christmas shopping. You will be as thrilled as the small fry when you see LAUGHING GIANT'S vast array of wonder toys, plus all the old favorites.

<u>Hundreds of Specials for Our Opening</u>
<u>Celebration—Oct. 16th through 23rd!</u>
<u>Free Favors! Free Soda Pop!</u>

Mark the dates on your calendar, and be here for the ribbon-cutting ceremony at 10 o'clock October 16th if you can. Beautiful Miss Suburbantown will do the honors, helped by two very funny clowns and your own store manager. We are looking forward to greeting you.

Yours truly,

John Doe, Mgr.
SUBURBANTOWN LAUGHING GIANT

#222   (Letterhead)

September 3, 19___

Mrs. Edward Jones
1129 Pleasant St.
Anytown, Nev. 00000

Dear Mrs. Jones:

Here's some exciting news for all the discriminating folk who love gourmet foods . . . who like to lift everyday menus out of the ordinary with a dash of distinction . . . or put forth a party buffet that will be the talk of the town. You can now pick up your gourmet goodies along with your regular groceries. Come see! Come savor!

Big Volume Super Markets
OPEN A GOURMET FOOD DEPARTMENT
in Every Big Volume Store
Starting September 5th!

Gala Opening in Your Neighborhood B.V. Monday, with Free Samples, Special Buys!

Plan now to join the fun. Look for the colorful red-and-white canopy with the big sign that says GOURMET FOODS. Let our hostess ply you with rare tidbits. Take advantage of opening savings on everything from barbecued almonds to imported escargots to smoked turkey. Hundreds of exciting finds line the shelves. We're expecting you!

Yours very truly,

YOUR B.V. STORE MANAGER

You Can Have Dignity with Sell

When the character of your business dictates dignity in your advertising, you can still put selling power into an announcement. Here are two examples:

#223   (Letterhead)

June 23, 19___

Mr. Joseph Bently
Eminent Jewelry Co.
2904 Prestige St.
Bigtown, Neb. 00000

Dear Mr. Bently:

With an eye to profit, considerable diversification is now being planned by many leading jewelry stores throughout the country. Blank Bros. Wholesale Jewelers, ever alert to new trends, wishes to announce an important addition to our stocks.

Beginning Now, Blank Bros. Will Offer
a Complete Line of Elite Co.
SMALL ELECTRICAL APPLIANCES.

These are not ordinary electrical appliances, but a line of superior quality and beauty, many of which will grace the finest tables. Included are coffee urns, hot trays, chafing dishes, and such, in addition to mixers, blenders, etc. You will find the complete line pictured on pages 239 through 251 of our new catalog, which should have already reached you. We are happy to say that we have a complete stock of these beautiful pieces, so that you may order in quantity now for immediate delivery or for the Christmas season.

Our usual discount applies to prices shown.

Very truly yours,

John Blank, Vice-Pres.

The following dignified announcement is brief and to the point, yet manages to do a bit of selling, somewhat in the style of the telephone company.

#224   (Letterhead or card)

April 4, 19___

ANNOUNCING A CHANGE IN BILLING DATES

In line with our policy of streamlining our operation wherever possible, in order to decrease costs, we are making a change in our billing dates, as explained below. The savings accomplished are important to you, because such savings are always passed on to Blank & Co. customers in the form of lower prices.

Beginning May 1, 19___, Blank & Co. statements will be sent out on staggered dates, so that the work of making out the statements can be spread out over the entire month. The date of your billing is decided by the initial of your last name or your firm name. Please make a note of your new billing date as indicated here:

Names Beginning With:

A, B, C, D, E, F, or G—1st and 2nd of Month

H, I, J, K, L, M, N—5th and 6th of Month

O, P, Q, R, S—15th and 16th of Month

T, U, V, W, X, Y, Z—20th and 21st of Month

Our usual payment terms remain in effect. Payment is requested within 10 days of your individual billing date. If you have any question about the new arrangement, please call your customer representative. She will be happy to explain all details. Thank you.

                 (Signed)   <u>H.P. Blank</u>, President

The next announcement came in the mail as this chapter was being written. It serves its major purpose very well, but it could have carried a business-building message in addition. This would have helped defray the cost of labor, paper and postage.

#225   RICHARD ROE INSURANCE AGENCY

<u>WE'RE MOVING</u>
To Serve You Better In Larger Offices Just Down The Street.

EFFECTIVE MARCH 16TH OUR NEW ADDRESS WILL BE

<u>2721 ADAMS AVENUE</u>
<u>BIGTOWN, OH. 00000</u>
(Easy Access from Freeway 00)

<u>SAME TELEPHONE NUMBER:—000-0000—</u>24 HOURS A DAY

Stop by any day except Sunday, between 10:00 A.M. and 1:00 P.M., and we'll have a cup of coffee while we talk.

KINDEST REGARDS,

RICHARD ROE INSURANCE AGENCY

An additional short paragraph at the end, before the signature, might start some customer thinking. It could bring in a little extra business immediately, or at the least contribute to a long-term sales campaign. Suggested addition:

Remember, as an independent insurance agent, I am not restricted to one company. Together we can go over a wide range of policies, and select the one best suited to your needs.

Using Letters for Holiday Greetings

Christmas cards are beautiful and traditional, but sometimes a letter can be used very effectively to carry your greetings to your customers. In a way it is more personal, and you can say more. Letters have a practical angle, too. Even though you may have your letter decorated and illuminated, and enclosed in a red envelope, it will probably turn out to be less expensive than a Christmas card.

Here are some interesting holiday letters:

#226   (Special Letterhead)

Christmastime, 19___

Mr. James R. Smith, Mgr.
Parts Dept.
Aeronautics Co.
4709 Outlying Road
Anytown, Calif. 00000

Re: This Important Season.

Dear Jim:

We could send you a programmed greeting. More and more the world is being run electronically. That's good most of the time, for your business and ours. But as much as we are sold on the speed and the marvels of this computerized age, somehow we become old-fashioned in one area at Christmas-time. That's where our friends are concerned. . . .

Something human and warm in the heart takes over, at this season and we take time out to wish you a besutiful, bountiful, sentimental

MERRY CHRISTMAS AND HAPPY NEW YEAR!

(Signed)   John Doe

And all of us at Electronics Co.

#227   (Giant, outsize letterhead)

December 20, 19___

Miss Jennie Brown, Buyer
Better Dress Dept.
Important Store
Anytown, Pa. 00000

Dear Miss Brown:

It takes something bigger than a card to express our thanks for your patronage during the wonderful year just past, and so we have tried to cut our cloth accordingly.

We have had to go into extra sizes, too, to accommodate the warmth and the huge scope of our good wishes to you during this holiday season:

SEASON'S GREETINGS
and HAPPY NEW YEAR!

(Signed)   Sam Blumenstein

BETTER GARMENT MFG. CO.

The next letter was printed in enlarged red and green typewriter type on a brown paper bag.

#228

December 21, 19___

Mr. Alex Jones, Mgr.
Supply Dept.
Suburban Markets
Bigtown, N.J. 00000

Dear Alex:

This is not Santa's bag we're sending you (we wish it were), but it carries a huge load of thanks for our happy association during the year just past.

And it is topped off with a giant order of heartfelt good wishes for you and yours.

MERRY CHRISTMAS AND HAPPY NEW YEAR!

From the Whole Gang at Double-Bag Co.

(Signed)   Joe Smith

───

CHAPTER 13

Writing Meaningful

Thank-You Letters

Thank-you letters are one of the graces that make business routine tolerable, even pleasurable. They are absolutely essential to maintaining good relationships, and their neglect can hurt you. It is better to give too many thanks (if that is possible), than too few Whenever you *feel* appreciative, sit down and write about it. A word of thanks is little enough to give in return for extra effort, extra concern that some conscientous or generous associates extend.

No great skill is involved in writing a good thank-you letter. The main point is that the letter should seem genuine and artless. Toward this end, it is wise to write your thank-you letter when the thought first occurs to you, when you remember with pleasure what was done for you. Mention a few definite things that pleased you.

Here are some good thank-you letters that should inspire you and start your thoughts percolating:

#229   (Letterhead)

July 12, 19___

Mr. Richard Roe, President
Richard Roe & Co., Inc.
2929 Business St.
Anytown, Mich. 00000

Dear Mr. Roe:

Your Westfield plant is truly a marvel. I don't think I have ever seen such an efficient, smooth-running operation. This is apparent at all stages, but I was particularly impressed with the inspection processes. Thank you for giving me the opportunity of observing all this at closehand.

I thoroughly enjoyed my tour and the delicious luncheon at the Stag & Hound afterward. All your employees deserve thanks for their courtesy and patience, but I want especially to commend Mr. Burton. He is a delightful host, and he certainly knows every angle involved in metal fabrication.

I made notes on my tour and I shall use the facts in my presentation. I will let you know what develops.

With very best regards,

#230   (Letterhead)

July 12, 19___

Mr. John Burton, Mgr.
Richard Roe & Co., Inc.
111 Outlying St.
Westfield, Ill. 00000

Dear Mr. Burton:

I want to thank you again for the informative and very enjoyable day you provided me when I visited the Westfield plant. I have just written Mr. Roe also to express my appreciation for the courtesies extended to me, and to tell him how impressed I was with the breadth of your knowledge. I could not have had a better guide or a more delightful host.

Sincerely,

The next is a more restrained, less personal type of letter

#231   (Letterhead)

May 4, 19___

Mr. John Doe, Sales Mgr.
Doe Printing Co.
1020 Anystreet
Bigtown, N.J. 00000

Dear Mr. Doe:

I want to thank you for the privilege of taking my group on the guided tour through your giant offset plant in Hackensack. I feel that the knowledge we gained will enable our people to produce better work, with fewer changes necessary, and will make for a smoother operation all around. The tour was an excellent idea, and I commend you. I will be in touch with you soon.

Yours very truly,

J.C. Blank, Adv. Mgr.

Model Letters for Other Situations

#232   (Letterhead)

January 9, 19___

Mr. J.J. Graham
John Doe Co.
3109 Business St.
New York, N.Y. 00000

Dear Mr. Graham:

I want to thank you and your lovely wife for inviting me to your home during my visit to New York. I was honored, and I thoroughly enjoyed myself as well. Mrs. Graham is a gourmet cook! I have dined in fine restaurants all over the world, but I have never before eaten Beef Stroganoff so delicious. Everything, in fact was perfectly prepared; and the Cherries Jubilee made a magnificent finish. Tell your wife for me that she has spoiled me for ordinary fare.

Going from the sublime to the mundane, my plane was held up by fog for twelve hours at Chicago, wrecking my schedule here. I have not been able to get another appointment with Mr. Darling until the 25th, and so I have no word yet on the proposal we discussed. I feel optimistic, however, and will let you know results as soon as I can.

With warmest regards,

The above letter would probably suffice as thanks to Mrs. Graham in most circles. The writer was punctilious, however, and he sent the proper handwritten note to Mrs. Graham.

#233   (Personal stationery or plain bond)

January 9, 19___

Dear Mrs. Graham,

I have just written your husband to tell him what a marvelous hostess you are, but I wish to convey my thanks to you personally for your wonderful hospitality. I have never in my life enjoyed a more delicious meal. The whole evening was delightful. Please know that I deeply appreciate all that you and Mr. Graham did to make my visit to New York so enjoyable.

Sincerely,

(Signed)   Ben Brown

The next letter is short and to the point, but certainly expresses appreciation. (If it is a personal letter the business address is omitted.)

#234   (Letterhead or personal stationery)

May 14, 19___

Mr. Henry Johnson
John Doe Co.
411 Business St.
Anytown, Ala. 00000

Dear Henry:

Thank you for your very excellent advice. You have convinced me. I deeply appreciate your concern and the time and trouble you went to in my interest. Please do not hesitate to call on me if there is anything I can do for you, now or in the future.

Sincerely,

(Signed)   Richard Roe

In conveying thanks for presents it is important to mention the name of the gift and to say something precisely applying to it—how it looks in the place you chose for it, how it feels, how it will serve you—whatever is appropriate to the particular item.

#235   (Letterhead)

June 23, 19___

Mr. George Jones
George Jones Co.
173 Mountain Road
Anytown, Wy. 00000

Dear George:

That is certainly one handsome desk set you sent me. Whenever I sit down at my desk it makes me feel like a wheel. Sometimes (when no one is around!) I lean over and smell the corners on the blotter, just to get a whiff of that real Morocco leather. You don't hardly get real leather no more! I am glad you chose green, too.

Thanks a million, George

You will be glad to know that things are going very well since the opening. Let's hope it keeps on that way. I'll give it my best.

With warmest regards,

_____

_____

#236   (Personal stationery)

June 28, 19___

Dear Mr. Roe:

Robert and I were simply thrilled with the gorgeous silver platter you sent me as a wedding present. It is quite the handsomest piece I own, and it goes perfectly with my flatware. I love the pierced border. Thank you for your thoughtfulness and generosity.

Sincerely,

(Signed)   Jean Black

_____

_____

#237   (Personal stationery)

December 29, 19___

Dear Mr. Roe:

Robert and I wish to thank you for the beautiful onyx bookends you gave us for Christmas. They look simply stunning on top of his new desk, holding his business books. I confess I opened the gift before Christmas, and when I saw the bookends I bought a desk lamp with an onyx base. The two things are like a set. We just love the effect.

We had a wonderful Christmas, and hope you did, too. Happy New Year!

Sincerely,

(Signed)   Jean Black

_____

#238   (Letterhead or personal stationery)

December 29, 19___

Mr. Richard Roe
Richard Roe Industries
2912 Industrial Rd.
Anytown, Ind. 00000

Dear Mr. Roe:

Thank you, sir, for the Christmas bonus check. It will come in very handy at this time of year, but Anne and I are determined to bank part of it. We did buy a handsome lamp that is a present for both of us, and we will get much enjoyment out of that.

We hope you had a fine Christmas. Your check helped to make ours a great one. Happy New Year from both of us!

Yours very truly,

Clement Brown

#239 is a letter of thanks for a not so usual service.

#239   (Letterhead)

January 14, 19___

Anonymous Safety Engineering Assoc.
4115 Any St.
Anytown, Ind. 00000

Dear Sirs:

Practical Toy Co. and I wish to express our appreciation for the A.S.E.A. Safety Award and certificate that you presented to us for the year just past. I cannot think of any honor that I would rather have for our company. In addition, of course, the reference to the award in our advertising will be a matter of pride and profit.

Be assured that we will continue to try to meet the standards set up by
A.S.E.A. We are in complete agreement with your aims.

Yours very truly,

Richard Roe, President
Practical Toy Co.

Thank-You Letters with a Dual Purpose

Some thank-you letters are sincerely meant, and are necessary
in business, but they have a happy way of enhancing certain business
relationships. Note these examples:

#240   (Letterhead)

March 3, 19___

Miss Rose Milton
Big Store
Bigtown, Ky. 00000

Dear Miss Milton:

The models you selected went out today under my personal supervision.
Thank you for your order. I want you to know that I truly enjoyed my
visit with you. I hope this is the beginning of a long and profitable
association for both of us.

You will find that M & J's regular line moves quickly, but M & J is always
ready to work with you on special events and seasonal promotions. Don't
forget.

Next time you are in our town stop by M & J early, if you can, and let me
take you to lunch. I know a great little Italian place, if you like Italian
food. Or you make the choice.

With very best regards,

#241   (Letterhead or personal stationery)

June 9, 19___

Dr. Margaret Brown
John Doe Laboratories
6912 Business St.
Anytown, Kans. 00000

Dear Dr. Margaret:

I am most grateful to you for referring me to Dr. Bentley. I found, as you said, that he had done an immense amount of research on the nature of crystals, and he was most generous in sharing it with me. As soon as he heard your name, I was his friend. He is a grand person as well as a great scholar, and we hit it off very well.

I don't know how I can ever thank you enough for what this association has meant to me. As a poor token, I am sending you one of my cymbidiums—a choice one. I hope you like it. You will find it does very well as a house plant, with a little care. I typed and enclosed instructions on its culture. I hope the orchid arrives in good condition. Please let me know if it does not, and I will replace it.

Again, thank you.

Sincerely,

(Signed)   Alan

#242   (Letterhead)

February 4, 19___

Mr. George Vandever
305 Main St.
Bigtown, Ga. 00000

Dear Mr. Vandever:

This is just a note to tell you how much I enjoyed my visit with you Thursday. I had no idea I would find another trimaran enthusiast here in landlocked Bigtown!

I took your advice on revising my presentation and I think it will do me some real good. If I may, I should like to stop in and show you what I have done. I will telephone first to make sure you are free.

Yours very truly,

Southeast Sales Dept.

Thank-You While Asking Another Favor

#243   (Letterhead)

May 3, 19___

Mr. William Jones
220 Outlying St.
Bigtown, Io. 00000

Dear Mr. Jones:

I had you paged at your hotel and at the airport, but I was unsuccessful in reaching you before you left. You've guessed it. I have another favor to ask. It completely slipped my mind while you were here, but we not only need the S49 part you are going to have specially machined for us, but we need a replacement for the Y742 lever on the collater. We cannot possibly get that rush job under way without it. Do you suppose you could locate one? And send it at the same time as the other part?

I know I was imposing on you when I asked the first favor. And now this! All I can tell you is that I am deeply grateful for your mercy and generosity. If I don't get those parts in place before the 15th I will be sunk, and our short and beautiful association at Richard Roe Co. will die on the vine.

With many thanks for your patience and cooperation,

John Doe, Supervisor
Supplies & Maintenance Div.

#244   (Letterhead)

April 5, 19___

Mrs. Natalie Gordon, Adv. Mgr.
Leading Mercantile Co.
Suburbanville, N.Y. 00000

Dear Mrs. Gordon:

You were so kind to send me all the photos and plans you used for setting up the flea market in your parking lot. I feel sure that with all this information our people should be able to put together a pretty fair imitation. I am deeply grateful.

Will you forgive me if I ask for more help? I now realize that the physical aspect of the flea market is only half the story, and I have only the vaguest notion of how to promote the affair. I think you said you used teaser advertising. If it is not too much trouble, I wonder if you could send me some copies of your ads—or tell me the dates of tear sheets I might send for. Also, since you have been so successful in recruiting participants, do you suppose I might have a copy of your letter to the various women's organizations?

Again, please forgive me for being such a pest, but promotion of this sort is entirely new to me. I hope that at some time in the future I can do something to assist you. Please do not hesitate to call on me if you can think of anything at all that I might do.

John Doe, Adv. Mgr.
LITTLE STORE CORP.

Thank You, But You Did Not Do It Right

Sometimes you have a valuable connection with a company or a person, and they do a great deal for you, yet you find yourself in the awkward position of having to say that the service is unsatisfactory. The following two letters cover such situations tactfully.

#245   (Letterhead)

March 21, 19____

Mr. John Doe
Parts Div.
Modern Industrial Co.
1604 Distant Rd.
Bigtown, Oh. 00000

Dear Mr. Doe:

I know you went to a great deal of trouble to find something suited to our purposes, and I appreciate it; however, the models you sent just won't do. They would never pass the stress test for our high-powered machine. I am returning them, marked for your attention.

Why don't you forget the whole darned thing for the time being. I am sure there will be other occasions, and fairly soon, when we can work with you. Please keep in touch. And thank you again for your efforts this time around.

Yours very truly,

Parts Procurement Div.

#246   (Letterhead)

September 16, 19____

Mr. William Johnson
Quality Manufacturing Co.
3724 Industrial Rd.
Outlying Town, Mich. 00000

Re: Sample Shipment of July 31. Temporary Inv. #97543128

Dear Mr. Johnson:

Thank you for acting so promptly on our request. However—and I hate to tell you this—the very important miniaturized components we discussed were omitted from the shipment.

Will you please see what you can do to get these to me as soon as possible? (A list is enclosed.) Fortunately I was able to hold off on my appointment with Mr. Jones, but I don't want to delay too long. The opportunity could pass.

With best regards,

Enc.

#247 (Letterhead)

April 14, 19___

Ms. Rita Roe
1525 Residential St.
Metropolis, N.Y. 00000

Dear Rita,

I have dreaded writing this letter, but I must. Your beautiful drawings arrived yesterday, but we cannot use them. If you will refer to my instruction sheet you will note that I specified <u>dry brush</u> for this art, and you have done the figures in wash. What happened?

As you can appreciate, I can't stick three wash figures on a page that has everything else in dry brush—at least when it is not planned that way. Unfortunately the time is so short now that I cannot wait to have you do the figures over. I will just have to pick up some old art and have it doctored here.

I am sorry you wasted all that work. I will try to make it up to you in the next couple of months. Please stop in and see me the next time you are in town.

Sincerely,

Jane Doe
ART DIRECTOR

The art director who wrote the above letter was furious and disappointed when she received the unusable drawings referred to. It would have been easy for her to write an angry, critical letter; but she took care not to. She wanted to continue to use this first-class artist's work, and not alienate her.

CHAPTER *14*

Personal Letters in a

Business Framework

Since a third of our adult lives and more is spent in a business environment, many of the people we deal with become almost as close to us as our own families. When someone gets married, when a child is born, when someone dies . . . these great events in the lives of our friends call for expressions of our feelings. Greeting cards may do very well for lighter occasions like birthdays, but for momentous happenings no canned verse can take the place of a personal letter. The mere fact that you took the time to write is tremendously important.

Such letters need not be long, or clever, although those celebrating happy occasions may be witty or unusual if you have a talent for it. Some letters, as noted in the models given, should be handwritten on personal stationery. Most, of course, may be typed

256

Congratulations on Opening a New Business

#248 (Letterhead)

May 3, 19___

Mr. William Green
Spectrum Sporting Goods
1912 Busy St.
Anytown, Mo. 00000

Dear Bill,

Well, you finally did it! Congratulations on the opening of your new sporting goods store. I can't wait to get over and see it. I might even make a purchase! How's your stock of mumbletypeg equipment?

All kidding aside, Bill, I think you are wonderful for having the courage to strike out on your own. Lots of guys talk about doing this all their lives and never make the move. You have done it, gotten it all together, and I am sure your business will be a great success.

Give my regards to Marge. I bet she is proud of you. I hope to see you both at the new store next Saturday.

With warmest regards,

(Signed)   Jim

#249 (Letterhead)

February 14, 19___

Mr. John Baker
Baker Industrial Extrusions
914 Industrial Rd.
Bigtown, Ala. 00000

Dear Baker:

I just received the announcement regarding the opening of Baker Industrial Extrusions. Congratulations! There is certainly no one in the field who knows more about it than you do, and there is room for another company. I wish you every success.

Sincerely,

J.W. Smith

#250   (Letterhead)

September 3, 19___

Mr. R.B. Bradley
Management Consultants
412 Broad St.
Bigtown, N.J. 00000

Dear Bradley:

I just saw the story in *The Wall Street Journal* about your opening your own consulting firm. I think it's great, and I want to congratulate you. Write and tell me details, or send me a brochure when you get the time.

With all good wishes,

Henry M. Marshall

#251   (Letterhead)

March 14, 19___

Ms. Mae Jones
Advertising Expertise
1711 Prestige St.
Metropolis, Calif. 00000

Dear Mae:

You are the envy of all of us poor working stiffs. I think you are marvelous, getting the capital together and opening your own agency. With your talent and your outstanding personality I am sure you will be a great success. Please accept my congratulations.

Sincerely,

(Signed)   Ben

Congratulations for Honors, Awards

#252   (Letterhead)

May 3, 19___

Dear Harry,

I just saw the news in the morning paper that your daughter Nancy took first prize in the regional Science Fair. Wonderful! You must be very proud. I am astounded that any child her age could do such a detailed study of genetic tendencies. Question: How come you never told me you had a genius in the family? And a beautiful one, at that?

Best—

(Signed)   Bill

#253   (Letterhead)

June 10, 19___

Mr. Henry Brown, Comptroller
Miscellaneous Corporation
1020 Industrial St.
Bigtown, Mont. 00000

Dear Mr. Brown:

I just heard the news. Please accept my congratulations on your election to
the Board. I am sure the company will benefit from your wisdom and
experience, and from your progressive outlook.

Respectfully,

James Stevens
Distributing Div.

#254   (Letterhead or personal stationery)

July 10, 19___

Dr. Richard Roe
Nuclear Research Laboratories
Midwestern University
1111 College Lane
Smalltown, Ind. 00000

Dear Dr. Roe:

Allow me to congratulate you, sir, on your having received the Smithson
Award. I know of no one more deeply deserving of the honor, and I am
happy to know that you will be able to continue your epoch-making
research. All mankind will benefit.

Very truly yours,

#255 (Letterhead)

ᵀanuary 9, 19___

Mr. Henry Jackson, Sales Mgr.
Southeastern Div.
Miscellaneous Industries
1408 Busy St.
Bigtown, Ga. 00000

Dear Jackson:

I wish to congratulate you personally for the achievements that brought you the President's Trophy. You and your staff have set a high mark for the other regional groups to shoot at.

With very best regards,

John Doe, Gen. Mgr.
MISCELLANEOUS INDUSTRIES

Congratulations on Marriages, Births, Adoptions

In the odd world of business, you may sometimes know someone, such as a salesman or a client, very well indeed, yet not have a social relationship that would put you on the list for a wedding announcement. Notwithstanding, you may want to express your warm feeling for him in a congratulatory letter. The following model letters cover a variety of important personal events.

#256 (Letterhead or personal note paper)

June 27, 19___

Dear Jim,

I have heard the news of your marriage, and I want to congratulate you. I think it's great that you have tied the knot, and I hope this means you can have your children with you again.

Please tell the new Mrs. Brown that she is a lucky lady to have found such a wonderful guy. I wish you both every happiness.

Sincerely,

(Signed)   Jane Doe

#257   (Letterhead or personal note paper)

March 3, 19___

Dear Myra,

I received the announcement of the birth of little Gloria. What wonderful news, and how happy you and your husband must be. I am sure your daughter will be a beautiful and gifted person, considering the parents she chose. Please send us a picture as soon as you can.

With warmest regards,

(Signed)   Marion

#258   (Letterhead)

January 14, 19___

Dear Dick,

I just heard the news of the birth of the future President of the United States. Congratulations to you and Mrs. Smith. Everyone in the office is agog. Be sure to bring pictures on your next trip here.

With all good wishes,

(Signed)   Bill

#259 (Letterhead)

September 5, 19___

Dear Vivian,

So the great day finally came! Down at the Press office they told me you nearly set the place on fire when you got the news that the adoption was approved. I don't blame you. It is not everybody that can become an instant parent—but you deserve the honor. And you can tell little Ralph from me that he is a very fortunate baby to get such a fine mommy and daddy. Congratulations and all good wishes to the three of you.

Sincerely,

(Signed)   Jim

P.S. Send pix instantly!

#260 (Letterhead or personal note paper)

February 11, 19___

Dear Bea,

Congratulations, Grandmother! I just heard the wonderful news of your first grandchild's arrival, and I had to write you, even though we have not seen each other for years. I trust that mother and baby are doing well.

If you can tear yourself away from spoiling the new member of the tribe, please write me, and send some pictures.

With warmest regards,

(Signed)   Helen

Congratulatory Letters to Someone Retiring

Even though he may have looked forward to leisure years, the man who is retiring usually begins to feel like a fifth wheel or a discard before he gets out the door. The kindest thing you can do for him is to assure him that he will be missed.

#261   (Letterhead or personal stationery)

December 1, 19___

Dear Ed,

I don't know how we are going to get along without you around here, but that is beside the point. Congratulations on having reached that blessed day when you can start directing your own life.

The best thing I can think of to say at this great moment is "Bon Voyage," and I mean it, because I know you will be embarking on a dozen new ventures of your own in the years ahead. Keep us posted on your doings, Ed, and don't forget to join the lunch bunch now and then.

With warmest regards,

#262   (Letterhead or personal stationery)

June 1, 19___

Dear Jake,

Don't go too far away, now that you are on your own. You have been such a kingpin in this outfit that it may start falling apart. Stay near enough so that we can grab you, or at least holler for advice. In the meantime, enjoy your well-earned leisure. Have fun! (How I envy you.)

Sincerely,

Writing Meaningful Sympathy Letters

Of all the times when friendship and humanity should supersede business considerations, the occasion of a death in the family of someone you know is most important. Sympathy letters should be straightforward, human, and above all, kind. If you have any sort of friendly relationship with the bereaved you should write a note as soon as possible, preferably in your own hand. Even a poorly written personal note is far more suitable than a printed card.

Such letters should not be difficult, because they are written from the heart. The following letters will be useful as models. They cover many different degrees in warmth, based on your relationship with the bereaved, and apply to many different situations.

#263 (Plain bond or personal note paper)

October 4, 19___

Dear Walter,

I was shocked and saddened to read in this morning's paper that your daughter had succumbed to the injuries she suffered in the accident last week. How terrible it must be for you and your dear wife to lose your lovely and gifted daughter at such an early age. I know there is little comfort in words, but I do want you to know how deeply I feel for you. Please call on me if there is anything at all that I can do to help.

Sincerely,

The next letter is a type that might be written when there has been less personal involvement in your business association, although you may have dealt with Walter for years:

#264 (Letterhead or personal stationery)

October 4, 19___

Dear Walter: (Or "Dear Mr. Smith:")

We at Black & Co. were shocked and saddened to hear of the death of your lovely daughter. How terrible it must be for you and Mrs. Smith. I and my associates wish to extend our heartfelt sympathy. Please let me know if there is anything that I personally can do to assist you at this tragic time.

Sincerely,

Director of Marketing
BLACK & CO.

The Letter to the Wife or Husband of Someone Who Has Died

The first model letter given is a very simple one, based on the letter a famous scientist wrote to the widow of a former associate.

For all its brevity, it has a comforting quality, referring as it does to happy memories.

#265   (Personal stationery)

July 3, 19___

Dear Mrs. Doe,

I am writing to tell you I was greatly saddened to hear of Bob's death. I remember with pleasure our association when he assisted me on the 1969-1971 project. I admired him as a man and a scientist.

Sincerely,

The next three letters are more personal. They might be written to someone close to you in your own business, and should be written on plain bond or on personal stationery.

#266

October 9, 19___

Dear Howard,

I want you to know how deeply saddened I have been at contemplating your loss. I wish I knew something comforting to say to you. Helen was a lovely, lovely lady, who did more than her share to make this world a better place. (Or: whose very presence made this world a better place.) I count myself fortunate that I was privileged to know her.

Sincerely,

(Signed)   Jed

#267

January 3, 19___

Dear Ben,

I was shocked and profoundly grieved to hear of Bertha's death. Please accept my deepest sympathy. Bertha was such a grand person, and I know that you were very close. It must be terrible for you, and yet, for the years you did have together, you were blessed. I myself feel grateful for the privilege of having known her.

Sincerely,

(Signed)   Anne

#268

May 29, 19___

Dear Janice,

Please know that I share your grief at Tom's passing. He was a wonderful guy. I will remember always how kind he was, and yet how witty and clever, how full of laughter. I think he would have wanted his friends to remember him that way.

Please call on me, Janice, I beg of you, if there is anything at all I can do to help you, whether it is with tasks or advice. That's what friends are for.

Sincerely,

Condolences to an Official of Another Company

#269   (Letterhead)

March 19, 19___

Mr. John Doe, President
John Doe Corporation
2927 Busy Street
Anytown, Mass. 00000

Dear Mr. Doe:

My associates and I at Richard Roe Co. were saddened at the news of Mr. Smith's death, and we wish to extend our condolences to you and to the family. The wise counsel and good company of your Board Chairman will be sorely missed in this city's business circles. Mr. Smith had many admiring friends, and we were proud to be numbered among them.

Sincerely,

Letters to an Executive You Do Not Know Well, Concerning a Personal Loss

---

#270   (Letterhead)

April 4, 19___

Mr. Henry Anderson, Comptroller
Diversified Industries
1209 Broad Street
Metropolis, Calif. 00000

Dear Sir:

I and my entire staff were grieved to hear of your great loss. Please allow us to extend our condolences.

Yours very truly,

#271   (Letterhead)

November 7, 19___

Mr. Charles Black, Sales Manager
Anonymous Co.
Outlying City, Ill. 00000

Dear Sir:

I was shocked and grieved to hear of your great loss. Please allow me to extend my condolences. I remember so well the graciousness and charm of Mrs. Black when she accompanied you on your visit here last year. She was a great lady.

Sincerely,

Sympathy Letters for Two Other Situations

#272   (Personal stationery)

March 15, 19＿

Dear Miss Johnson,

You do not know me, and yet, as a friend of your mother's, I feel that I know you well. I hope you will accept my condolences at this sad time. I, and all those who loved and admired your mother, are deeply grieved at her passing. She was a wonderful person.

Please write or call me if there is anything at all that I can do for you—any business I can attend to, any problem I can assist in solving. I realize that you are alone now, and I want to help if I can. I know how proud your mother was of you, and how dearly she loved you. Please let me be your friend.

With affectionate regards,

(Signed)   Catherine Anderson

A Delayed Sympathy Letter

#273   (Personal stationery)

August 10, 19＿

Dear Don,

I have been abroad for several months, as you know, and only now learned of the death of your dear wife last June. I was shocked and saddened. Please accept this belated expression of sympathy.

I wish I could have been with you at the time, dear friend. It is terrible when one so charming and good dies so young, and yet I guess we have to be thankful that Kay was spared a life of suffering. I hope this thought has been some slight comfort to you.

I plan to be up your way early next week, and I will call you. I am taking an extra day, so that I can spend some time with you.

With warmest regards,

(Signed)   John

Replies to Letters of Condolence

Letters of condolence should be acknowledged, and they should be signed by the person who was addressed. The simplest wording will suffice for replies to formal letters such as #269 and #270. For example:

#274   (Letterhead or plain bond)

March 29, 19___

Mr. James Johnson, President
Richard Roe & Co.
Bigtown, Conn. 00000

Dear Mr. Johnson:

Your expression of sympathy on the death of our Board Chairman, Mr. Henry B. Smith, is much appreciated.

Sincerely,

Alternate wording:

Thank you for your very kind expression of sympathy. Mr. Smith often spoke of you. He held you in high regard, both as friend and business associate.

Sincerely,

Replies to more personal sympathy letters may be just as brief. Some examples:

#275 (Personal stationery)

November 20, 19____

Dear Mr. Jones:

Your kind expression of sympathy was greatly appreciated.

Sincerely,

#276 (Personal stationery)

October 20, 19____

Dear Jed,

Thank you for your beautiful letter upon the occasion of Helen's death. I found your words very comforting.

Sincerely,

#277 (Personal stationery)

March 28, 19____

Dear Miss Anderson,

Your expression of sympathy in regard to the death of my mother was deeply appreciated. Mother considered you one of her dearest friends, and your kind letter to me was heartwearming. I want to thank you, too, for your offer of assistance. It is good to know that I can call on you if the need arises.

Sincerely,

Letters to the Sick and Injured

There are times when the patient's condition is so serious that cheery or amusing get-well cards are inappropriate. A note expressing your concern will be more thoughtful, and will be appreciated. In such communications it is best to generalize about the patient's illness or injuries, so as not to alarm him. Do not mention anything that he may not have been told. Here are several examples of letters that seem straightforward, yet say nothing that might be unwise.

#278   (Letterhead or personal stationery)

January 12, 19___

Dear Jim,

I called your office today to add a couple of items to our order and was astounded to hear that you are in the hospital. I am so sorry, Jim. But with your toughness and the skills the doctors have nowadays I know that you will soon be well. Take it easy, and don't try to rush things. I hope to visit you soon.

With warmest regards,

#279   (Letterhead or personal stationery)

April 3, 19___

Dear Bill,

I was so very sorry to hear of your accident. Everybody is going to miss you around here—but don't you worry about that. You take your time and get thoroughly mended.

I am going to try to get over to see you on Friday. Tell June to let me know if there is anything you would especially like me to bring you, and if there is anything you would like me to do for you. In the meantime, be a good patient and help the M.D.'s to get you well soon.

Best—

#280 (Letterhead or personal stationery)

May 16, 19___

Dear Mr. McNeil:

I looked for you at the North Shore Merchants' meeting today, and then Howard Burns told me of your illness. I was shocked, of course, but I know you will lick this thing.

If it had to happen, it is good that you picked the slow season, so you won't be tempted to get back into action too soon. As you know, you have Johnson so well-trained that he will keep things going like clockwork. Incidentally, the Merchants' Association approved your plan for decorating Shore Street next fall. Dan Buckley is going to take care of details.

Please know that everyone is concerned for you, and that you have all my best wishes for a speedy recovery.

Sincerely,

#281 (Letterhead)

November 2, 19___

Dear Miss Smith:

Your sister called me this morning to tell me that you are in the hospital. I was very sorry to hear such news, and I hope that you will soon be well. I want you to concentrate on that right now. Do not worry about the office. We will manage somehow, and your job will be waiting for you when you are ready and fully recovered.

Everyone I have talked to expresses concern for you, and you know that you have my best wishes. Take care of yourself.

Sincerely,

Fancy composition and clever ideas are unimportant in these letters. The main thing is that they should seem spontaneous and sincere.

CHAPTER 15

Guidelines for Good Appearance and

Other Technical Aspects of Letters

The way your letter looks is almost as important as the messege it carries. The first impression, which depends on appearance, often decides whether a letter will get immediate action or will be set aside. Good arrangement and use of type also help readability, and can clarify your message.

A little advance planning on the part of the typist turns the trick. The first thing to determine is whether the letter can be nicely placed on one page, or will run to two or more pages. The great majority of business letters will require but one page, especially if single-spaced.

Planning the Appearance of the One-Page Letter

Oddly enough, these single-page letters require the most planning; but the planning is not difficult. Just keep in mind this simple rule:

The shorter the letter, the wider the margins.

This rule will help you finish up with a letter that is well-placed on the page, with pleasing margins at top, sides and bottom.

If the letter which has been dictated consists of only three or four short sentences, set your side margins at 1½ or 1 3/4 inches, then drop down an inch or more below the letterhead imprint to type the date. When you do this, the letter will end up as a compact, well-proportioned type mass that is nicely framed in white space.

There is good scientific basis for typing short letters to narrower measure. Studies have shown that type lines which are too long in proportion to the depth of the type mass are actually hard to read. Perhaps this is why a short letter that is placed like a narrow speckled ribbon across the top of the page is so unprepossessing.

The body of a very short letter may be double-spaced, if you wish. In this case you would single-space the name and address of the addressee, and drop down at least three spaces before the salutation. You would also triple-space between paragraphs.

A one-page letter of several moderately lengthy paragraphs usually looks better if it is single-spaced, with double-spacing between paragraphs. If the letter is quite long, margins may be narrowed to 1¼ inches. As a rule, making margins narrower than this is not pleasing. The bad proportion of type to white space makes the letter look like a formidable reading task. Rather than making the margins too narrow, it is usually better to replan the design of the letter for two pages.

Break Up Paragraphs, Use Underlining If Appropriate

In typing the body of the letter, try not to have a single-spaced paragraph that is more than an inch and a half deep. Double-spaced paragraphs begin to look forbidding if they are more than three inches deep. (On practically all typewriters there are six lines to the inch.) You can usually divide a very long paragraph into two shorter ones, without even changing a word.

When it is appropriate, you can sometimes use tabulation of listings to make the letter more interesting looking. A discreet use of underlining, when appropriate, can also lend pleasing contrast.

Planning a Letter of More Than One Page

If a letter is too long for one page, use a plain sheet of paper for the second and succeeding pages. These plain sheets should be of the same quality as the letterhead. Plan your typing so that at least three lines of the letter go on the second page, before the complimentary closing.

Which Letter Format or Style Should You Use?

Most businesses require that all outgoing letters be typed in one format. If you have the choice, the block style is recommended, both for appearance and for practical reasons. On occasions when you must use tabulations, listings or inset portions, the neat block paragraphs keep the letter more orderly looking. The block style is but one of several generally accepted styles. They include the following:

BLOCK: No paragraphs are indented. Dateline and complimentary closing are lined up far to the right.

SEMI-BLOCK: Paragraphs are indented uniformly, from five to ten spaces, according to preference. Dateline and complimentary closing are aligned at far right.

FULL-BLOCK: Nothing is indented. All lines begin flush with the left margin. This form saves a little time in typing, perhaps, but loses esthetically.

INDENTED: This is rather old-fashioned. The date is placed far to the right. The first line of the address is flush with the left margin, but each succeeding line is indented five spaces more than the preceding line. The salutation is flush with the left margin, but all paragraphs are indented five spaces or more. The complimentary closing is usually centered.

SIMPLIFIED: This style is recommended by the Administrative Management Society, but I feel that it is one more step toward depersonalization and away from small courtesies in a highly mechanized era. In this letter form, a subject line is used in place of the salutation, and the complimentary close is omitted. The dictator's initials are omitted, but the typists initials, cc (for carbon copy) and *Enclosure* may be used.

VARIATIONS of many sorts may be used in advertising letters. One style, sometimes called *Hanging-Indented,* is seen quite frequently. In this the dateline, address, salutation, and complimentary closing are arranged as in a block style letter; but the paragraphs are different. The first line of each paragraph begins at the left margin, with succeeding lines in the paragraph indented uniformly by five spaces or more.

L E T T E R H E A D   I M P R I N T

June 3, 19__

Mr. John R. Carlson, Operations Manager
Miscellaneous Business Corp.
1011 Broad Street
Bigtown, Kansas 00000

Dear Mr. Carlson:

It was a pleasure being able to demonstrate for you the
smooth operation and other features of Blank Corp.'s new
Convenience Copier #364. I believe this model fits your
needs to a T. The fact that anyone can run it is so important, and I think you will find the patented jam-proof
feed a delight on those rush jobs you told me about.

I am enclosing the price information and detailed specifications you requested. As you will note, you can either
purchase the machine outright, rent it, or secure it on
the rent-buy option plan. Whichever way you choose, you
will find that the cost is amazingly low compared to other
machines. I will stop by in a day or so to go over with
you in detail the advantages of the various financial ar-
rangements -- I will call you first.

In the meantime, it you have any questions at all, please
telephone me at 000-0000. Our operator can always reach
me within a short time.

Yours very truly,

Richard N. Roe

Enclosure

Figure 1—The Popular Block Style

L E T T E R H E A D   I M P R I N T

March 12, 19__

Mr. Joel A. Blank, Purchasing Agent
General Suppliers Co.
3451 Industrial St.
Anytown, N.J.

Dear Joel

I thought I had missed you, then in checking over my customer
list the other day I noted that you had not been in for some
time. That probably means you are running low on some of
the staples you buy from us, and this is why I am writing
you.

We have just received notice from our suppliers that there
is going to be an across-the-board price increase for all
the S45 and L612 numbers that you use regularly. It just
happens that we have a fairly good supply of these right
now, and it occurred to me that you might want to buy ahead
in some quantity to save that extra 10%.

You know I am always ready to work with you on these things.
If it would suit your picture better, we probably could arrange to have a good part of your order scheduled for future
delivery. In any case, please let me know immediately what
your needs will be. Business has been good, and I don't
know how long our present stock will hold out. You can telephone or write me, of course, but I should rather see you.
There are some interesting new items for Apex that I think
you would like to look over.

If you do plan to come up here, let's plan to have lunch
together.

With Warmest Regards

Richard Roe & Co.

ar

cc: R. Roe, Henry Brown

Figure 2—Full Block style. Open Punctuation

L E T T E R H E A D   I M P R I N T

October 22, 19__

Mr. John Scott Fortune
1412 Opulent Avenue
Suburbantown, N.Y.   00000

A MESSAGE FOR LUXURY CAR OWNERS

There are many wonderful things about a big luxury car, but
parking downtown isn't one of them. One answer to the exas-
perating downtown parking situation might be a second car--
a special downtown car.

Our little car that loves leftovers can save a lot of
frazzled nerves. It's a great standby car, too, for occasions when the big car isn't on hand. Think about it.

A small investment in an agile little Volkswagen will solve
many problems. I'd like to show you some of the tricks it
can do in the downtown area -- in heavy traffic anywhere.
You can have a bug now with automatic transmissions or stick
shift; air conditioning, too.

Please jot on the enclosed card the most convenient time
for you to take a demonstration ride in our little pride
and joy -- day or evening. When I receive your card I will
telephone you and make an appointment to pick you up. There
is no obligation, of course.

JOE ENTERPRISE -- Anonymous Volkswagen Agency

mj

Enclosure

Figure 3—Simplified Style. Open Punctuation
is always used in this style.

Letters to Government Bureaus and the Military

Letters addressed to bureaus and departments of the Federal Government must conform to the rules of the agency addressed. Letters that do not conform to the requirements may be returned. This is especially true of the Military. Before sending any correspondence, write them for instructions, if your company does not already have such information on file.

Punctuating the Parts of the Letter

Most writers of business letters nowadays have eliminated all punctuation at the ends of the dateline and the address lines; however, a colon is used after the salutation, and a comma at the end of the complimentary close. You cannot go wrong with this usage, but many companies are adopting the use of so-called "open" punctuation, which eliminates even the colon after the salutation and the comma after the complimentary close.

If your company uses "open" punctuation, so be it; but I feel that such usage (or lack of usage) attracts so much attention to itself that it may actually detract from the impact of your letter. In sales letters and any letters that are attempting to create good will, it is better to be on the safe side and keep to more generally accepted customs. It is safe to say that no one will be irritated by the use of the colon and the comma in a well designed block form letter, but quite a few will be annoyed out of all proportion when these little marks are omitted.

What Abbreviations to Use

Use of standard abbreviations in the address are generally acceptable; however some companies rule against using abbreviations. State names are spelled out; words such as street, avenue and building are spelled out. Titles such as Vice President, Supervisor, Colonel, etc. are spelled out. Exceptions, of course, are Mr., Mrs., Ms., Dr., M.D., P.H.D. and similar familiar forms which are universally abbreviated. D.C., for District of Columbia, is never spelled out.

Unless your company has an ironclad rule against some abbreviations, there are certain terms that may be abbreviated or not, according to choice. These include:

- Prof. for Professor, Rev. for Reverend, and Hon. for Honorable, with one exception. When only the last name of the person is known, then the title must be spelled out, as Professor Jones, The Reverend Mr. Johnson, The Honorable Mr. Bailey.
- Business titles, such as Pres. for President, Sec. for Secretary, and Treas. for Treasurer.
- The name of a state, when it is part of an address.
- The names of thoroughfares, such as St. for Street, Ave. for Avenue, Rd. for Road, Blvd. for Boulevard.
- Words standing for points of the compass, when used in an address, such as E. for East, S. for South, N.W. for Northwest.

Abbreviating Names of States

As mentioned, the companies which object to abbreviations sometimes have a rule that state names be spelled out. It is well to note here that the Post Office prefers that volume mailers use their official abbreviations for state names. The use of Zip Code numbers is required. Pamphlets listing the correct Zip Codes and authorized state abbreviations can be obtained from the Post Office.

Corp. or Corporation?

In referring to an organization that has Corp. or Corporation as a part of its name, you must use the form of this word that is used in their letterhead. In other words, if the company's letterhead is imprinted Western Designers Incorporated, that is the way you should write the name. If they use J.C. Brown Sons, Inc., then you must do likewise. The same applies to Brothers or Bros. used in a company name.

Use of Titles

Some title in front of a name – Dr., Prof. or Professor, Mr., Mrs., or Miss – should always be used. (Ms. is still somewhat controversial. Use it or not, as you please.) On the other hand, there is a growing tendency to eliminate the use of such titles as Vice President, Superintendent, Editor, etc. following a name, except on the envelope. My thought is that people like their hard-earned titles, and it can do no harm to use them. When a person has two titles, try to use the more important one or the one that he himself prefers.

If the person to whom you are writing has an honorary title such as Dr., Prof. (Professor), or Dean, courtesy requires its use in the address line. When the title is used in the salutation, it should always be accompanied by the person's name. Examples:

Dr. John Doe
1020 Fourth St.
Anytown, Mich. 00000

Dear Dr. Doe: (Not "Dear Doctor:")

Prof. Rita Roe
Local State University
1103 Distant Road
Anytown, Minn. 00000

Dear Prof. Roe: or Dear Professor Roe: (Not "Dear Professor:")

In The United States, lawyers are given the honorary title of Esquire, but this is not placed in front of the name. On the envelope and in the address block of the letter, Esquire follows the name. Example:

Henry Jones, Esquire (or Henry Jones, Esq.)
Suite 105, Professional Building
1988 Busty St.
Anytown, Ind. 00000

Esquire is not used anywhere else in the letter. The salutation is simply "Dear Sir:" or "Dear Mr. Jones:".

Esquire is also used in the same manner for a clerk of the Supreme Court of the United States and for officers of other courts. It may also be used for foreign-service officers below the grade of career minister.

Using Military Titles

In the address on the envelope and inside the letter a military officer's complete title should be used. The title may be abbreviated when it is followed by the given name or initials and the surname, as: Brig. Gen. H.R. Smith.

The salutation is another matter. The salutation "Dear General Smith:" is used for brigadier generals, major generals, lieutenant generals, and generals. Similarly, lieutenant colonels and colonels are both given the salutation "Dear Colonel:". For rear admirals, vice admirals, full admirals and fleet admirals the correct form is "Dear Admiral Smith:". Retired officers of the armed forces are addressed in the same manner as when active.

When writing to an enlisted man in any of the services, use his abbreviated title plus his full name in the address block on the envelope and in the letter. On the second line write the branch of the service; followed by the designation of the military division on the third line. Example:

CMSgt. Richard Roe
Company A, Headquarters Wing U.S.A.F.
Kelly Air Force Base
San Antonio, Texas 00000

Further Pointers on Titles and Forms of Addresss

WIVES of men with titles are addressed as though there were no title. Gen. John Doe's wife would be addressed Mrs. John Doe, with the salutation Dear Mrs. Doe:.

WHEN ADDRESSED JOINTLY, the address line would read General and Mrs. John Doe; the salutation, Dear General and Mrs. Doe:. When a man is addressed as The Honorable, a letter to husband and wife would be addressed The Honorable and Mrs. Richard Roe. The salutation would be Dear Mr. and Mrs. Roe. In the case of the mayor of a city, the salutation to husband and wife would be Mayor and Mrs. Roe:.

HUSBANDS of women with titles are addresssed simply as Mr. John Doe. When husband and wife are addressed jointly, both envelope and inside address should read Mr. and Mrs. John Doe.

WOMEN with titles are addressed in the same manner as men with titles, but the salutation is Dear Madam or Madam, depending on the degree of formaility. Madam is more formal.

ACTING OFFICIALS—those appointed to act for another—should have the word "Acting" included in the address, if the title is used, as: Mr. John Doe, Acting President. The salutation would be simply Dear Mr. Doe or Dear Sir.

Reference List of Special Titles and Forms of Address

PERSON	HOW TO ADDRESS	SALUTATION
Alderman		
	Alderman Richard Roe	Dear Alderman Roe:
	The Honorable Richard Roe Alderman, City of Baltimore	Dear Mr. Roe:
Ambassador		
	The Honorable John Doe United States Ambassador Paris, France	Sir: Dear Mr. Ambassador: My dear Mr. (or Madam) Ambassador:
	For those with military title:	General John Doe
Archbishop		
	The Most Reverend John Doe	Your Excellency: Most Reverend Sir: Dear Archbishop Doe:
Associate Justice of U.S. Supreme Court		
	Mr. Justice Roe The Supreme Court Washington, D.C. 20543	Sir: My dear Mr. Justice: Dear Mr. Justice Roe:
Bishop (Catholic)		
	The Most Reverend Bishop Blank	Your Excellency: Dear Bishop Blank:
Bishop (Protestant)		
	The Reverend Bishop Blank or The Right Reverend Bishop Blank	Most Reverend Sir: My dear Bishop Blank:

PERSON	HOW TO ADDRESS	SALUTATION
Cabinet Member, U.S.		
	The Honorable Richard E. Roe Secretary of State Washington, D.C. 20520	Sir: Dear Mr. (or Madam) 　Secretary: Dear Mr. Roe:
Cardinal, U.S.		
	His Eminence, Richard 　Cardinal Roe Archbishop of Boston	Your Eminence: My dear Cardinal Roe:
Chaplain		
	Capt. John R. Doe (Ch. C.) 　U.S.N.	My dear Chaplain:
	Chaplain Richard Doe Captain, U.S.A.	My dear Chaplain Doe:
Chief Justice of the United States		
	The Chief Justice The Supreme Court Washington, D.C. 20543	Sir: My dear Mr. Chief Justice:
	The Honorable John R. Doe Chief Justice of the United 　States	
City Attorney		
	Hon. (or Mr.) Richard Roe City Attorney	Dear Mr. Roe:
Commissioner, City		
	The Honorable John R. Doe Commissioner of the City 　of Blank	Dear Mr. Doe:

PERSON	HOW TO ADDRESS	SALUTATION
Congressman		
	The Honorable Henry R. Blank House of Representatives Washington, D.C. 20515	Dear Representative Blank: My dear Mr. Blank:
	The Honorable Henry R. Blank Representative in Congress 0000 Central Street Anytown, Ka. 00000	
Consul		
	Mr. Richard Roe American Consul London, England	Dear Mr. Roe:
	In South and Central America: Consul of the United States of America	
County Supervisor		
	Hon. (or Mr.) John Doe Supervisor, San Diego County	Dear Mr. Doe:
Dean of a School		
	Dean John E. Doe School of the Arts New York University	Dear Dean Doe:
	Dr. Richard Roe Assistant Dean, School of Law University of Alabama	Dear Dr. Roe:
Delegate, Territorial; or Resident Commissioner		
	The Honorable Henry M. Blank House of Representatives Washington, D.C. 20515	My dear Mr. Blank:
District Attorney		
	The Honorable Richard L. Roe District Attorney, Orange County	Dear Mr. Roe:

PERSON	HOW TO ADDRESS	SALUTATION
Governor		
	The Honorable John C. Blank Governor of Pennsylvania Harrisburg, Pa. 00000	Sir: Dear Governor Blank:
Judge		
	The Honorable John Doe Judge of the District Court	Dear Judge Doe:
	The Honorable Rita Roe Judge of the Circuit Court	
Lieutenant Governor		
	The Honorable John R. Blank Lieutenant Governor of Montana Helena, Montana 00000	Sir: Dear Mr. Blank: My dear Governor Blank:
Mayor		
	The Honorable John R. Doe Mayor of San Diego San Diego, Ca. 00000	My dear Mayor Doe: Dear Mr. Mayor:
Minister		
	The Reverend John N, Doe	Dear Mr. Doe:
	The Reverend John N. Doe, D.D., Litt. D.	Dear Dr. Doe:
	The Very Reverend John N. Doe, D.D. Dean of St. John's Cathedral	Dear Dean Doe:
Monsignor		

	The Right Reverend Monsignor
	    Richard Roe
		The Right Reverend and
		    dear Monsignor:
		My dear Monsignor Roe:

Mother Superior		
	The Reverend Mother Superior Convent of the Sacred Heart	Reverend Mother: Dear Madam:

PERSON	HOW TO ADDRESS	SALUTATION
Nun	Mother Mary Louise, Superior Convent of the Sacred Heart	Dear Mother Mary Louise:
	Sister Anne Louise	Reverend Sister: Dear Sister Anne Louise:
Pope	His Holiness Pope Paul VI	Most Holy Father: Your Holiness:
President of a School	Dr. James Blank President, University of California	Dear Dr. Blank: Dear President Blank:
President of State Senate	The Honorable John Doe, President The Senate of New Mexico	Sir:
President of U.S. Senate	The Honorable Richard Roe President of the Senate Washington, D.C. 00000	Sir:
President of the United States	The President The White House Washington, D.C. 20500 The Honorable John N. Doe The White House Washington, D.C. 20500	Mr. President: My dear Mr. President:
Priest	The Reverend John Doe	Dear Reverend Father:

PERSON	HOW TO ADDRESS	SALUTATION
	The Reverend James Blank, Ph.D.	Dear Father Blank: Dear Dr. Blank:
Professor		
	Professor Richard E. Roe	Dear Mr. Roe:
	Dr. Richard E. Roe Associate Professor, Dept. of Chemistry	Dear Dr. Roe: Dear Professor Roe:
Rabbi		
	Rabbi Charles R. Blank	My dear Rabbi Blank:
	Dr. Charles R. Blank	My dear Dr. Blank:
	Rabbi Charles R. Blank, Ph.D.	
Secretary or Assistant to the President of the United States		
	The Honorable John B. Doe Secretary to the President The White House Washington, D.C. 20500	My dear Mr. Doe:
	General Richard Roe The Assistant to the President	My dear General Roe:
Senator, U.S. or State		
	The Honorable John C. Doe *Retired:*	My dear Senator Doe:
	The Honorable John C. Doe	My dear Mr. Doe:
Speaker of the House		
	The Honorable John Doe Speaker of the House of Representatives Washington, D.C. 20515	My dear Mr. Speaker:
State Legislator		
	The Honorable Richard E. Roe	Dear Senator Roe: Dear Mr. Roe:

PERSON	HOW TO ADDRESS	SALUTATION

State Officials

| | The Honorable John Doe
Secretary of State of Ohio | Sir:
My dear Mr. Secretary: |
| | The Honorable Richard Roe
Director of the Budget | Dear Mr. Roe: |

Under Secretary or
Assistant Secretary
(Federal Department.)

| | The Honorable John M. Blank
Undersecretary of State | My dear Mr. Blank: |
| | The Honorable John Doe
Assistant Secretary of Labor | My dear Mr. Doe: |

United Nations
Officials

	His Excellency John N. Doe
	Secretary General of the
	    United Nations
	United Nations
	New York, N.Y. 10021
		My dear Mr. Secretary
		    General:

	The Honorable John N. Doe Undersecretary of the United Nations	My dear Mr. Doe:
	His Excellency John N. Doe Representative of Great Britain to the United Nations	My dear Ambassador Doe:

	The Honorable John N. Doe
	United States Permanent
	    Representative
	    to the United Nations
		My dear Ambassador Doe:

Vice President of
the United States

| | The Vice President
United States Senate
Washington, D.C. 20510 | Sir: |
| | The Honorable John N. Doe
Vice President of the United
    States
Washington, D.C. 20501 | My dear Mr. Vice President: |

INDEX

INDEX